Beyond Sagebrush

Beyond Sagebrush

Secrets of Central Oregon's Natural World

Darin Furry

DF Publications, LLC
Bend, Oregon

Beyond Sagebrush
Secrets of Central Oregon's Natural World

Second Edition

Copyright © 2008, 2012 by Darin Furry

Photography, maps, and text by Darin Furry (except for credited photos)

Cover Design - Jody Conners

Graphics - George Goddard

Printing and Binding - Maverick Publications, Bend, Oregon

ISBN: 978-0-615-25213-1

Cover photo - Smith Rock with the Cascades in the background.

Back cover (top to bottom) - Lava Butte, Deschutes River Trail, Newberry Caldera

Contents

Acknowledgements

Some say writing a book is a lonely task. That's surprising, considering the number of people who helped me. I am grateful for their contributions because without them this book would never have been published.

Blame this book on Pat Barry. Years ago, he encouraged my interest in natural history education and helped me develop my writing skills.

For fact checking or tidbits of local knowledge, I sought help from professional biologists, meteorologists, and geologists. The employees of local U.S. Forest Service offices were incredibly helpful and generous with their time. I would like to thank David Baker, Rick Dewey, Andy Eglitis, Carrie Gordon, Katie Granier, Bob Jensen (retired), Dan Rife, and Lauri Turner for all their help. Jason McClaughry of the Oregon Department of Geology and Mineral Industries gave me information about the Crooked River Caldera. Bob Shaw of KTVZ helped me understand local meteorology.

Writing a book requires publishing expertise. I took a great class at COCC lead by Tom McDannold that taught me the ins and outs of publishing. Kate Haas, my editor, whipped my writing into shape. Gary Asher of Maverick Publications guided me through layout and printing. Thanks to George Goddard for his diagrams and the many people who graciously allowed me to use their photos. Keith Dodge helped answer questions about running a small business.

Greg Wilson and Lynn Wilson-Dean offered moral support, reviewed chapters, and gave advice whenever I asked (and I asked often!) Greg took all the aerial photographs.

Any errors, omissions, or political opinions in this book are solely the responsibility of the author and do not reflect upon the people (or their employers) whom I sought for input.

Welcome to Central Oregon

Where can you ski down a volcano, kayak a caldera, or choose to hike either above or below the ground? Central Oregon of course! This area is home to the largest juniper forest in the United States and one of the biggest organisms on the planet. We're surrounded by volcanoes, yet the largest and most powerful one remained hidden and was only recently discovered. UFO enthusiasts will love our "flying saucers," which are actually unusual, lens-shaped clouds. It's in a state famous for rainy weather, yet the climate is arid. Central Oregon is home to micro-tornado dust devils, a mini grand canyon, every known volcanic feature, ancient lake beds, toxic algae, the most deadly animal on the planet, and much, much more.

I love to explore. Whenever I travel or move to a new city, I see the sights and learn about the region. Exploring helps me develop a sense of place and appreciate what makes each area special. I've

Opposite page: Tumalo Falls.

never been disappointed, because every region is unique and exciting in its own way. Central Oregon is no exception.

As I explore, I'm awed at the variety and beauty around me. But the more I see, the more questions I have. Central Oregon is full of many wonderful and bizarre things. Why are there so many volcanoes here? Why do clouds suddenly appear in the desert on a summer day when no rain is forecast? Why do junipers form an open forest while lodgepole forests are dense? Where are all the animals?

I wrote *Beyond Sagebrush* to answer those questions and hope to fire your imagination and fuel your desire to explore. This book discusses Central Oregon's natural world and covers everything from climate and geology to plants and animals. Each chapter starts off with general information about a topic. Then I discuss things you can see and visit in Central Oregon, fascinating items in our region that will make you say "Wow!"

It's one thing to learn about something; but isn't it better to see it for yourself? The subjects in this book were carefully chosen with this in mind. I want you to go out, explore and see the things you've learned about. Each chapter contains a representative sample of subjects that are interesting, visible any time of the year, common

Hosmer Lake and Broken Top.

Exploring Smith Rock.

to the area, and easy to find. Depending on the topic, I provide driving directions (see appendix), identification tips, or the general region in which to find the subject. I tried my best to make it easy. For example, do you want to see a juniper tree? Almost all the trees along Highway 97 between Bend and Redmond are junipers.

The world is fun to explore. But you don't have to fly to another continent to experience the unusual or exotic. Many exciting things are right in front of you, stuff you see every day. Central Oregon is full of wonderful geologic features, interesting weather, and amazing plants and animals. So go out, learn, and see the sights. More importantly, have fun!

Geography of Central Oregon

Geography plays a huge role in Central Oregon. The mountains, hills, plains, and rivers all affect weather patterns, climate, and eco-systems and give the region its unique character. For example, Mt. Bachelor is renowned for its sunny ski slopes covered with dry powder. Geography plays a major role. Obviously, you need a mountain, and it needs to be tall enough so its upper slopes are in cool air. This allows snow to build up. The Cascades block wet weather from the Pacific and trap cold air from Canada, which give us our sunny weather and dry powder.

For the purposes of this book, I define Central Oregon as the area within roughly a fifty-mile radius of Bend. It stretches north-south from Madras to LaPine and west-east from the Cascade Mountains to Prineville Reservoir. The landscape alternates between plains and mountains. Rivers cut dramatic canyons, lined with steep-

Opposite page: Geography makes for good snow-boarding on Mt. Bachelor.

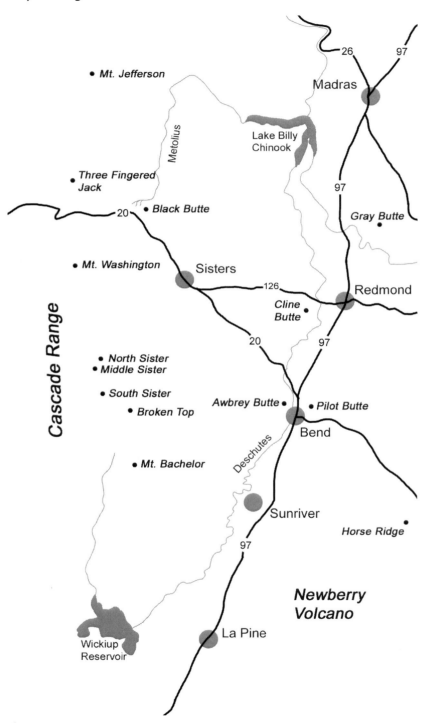

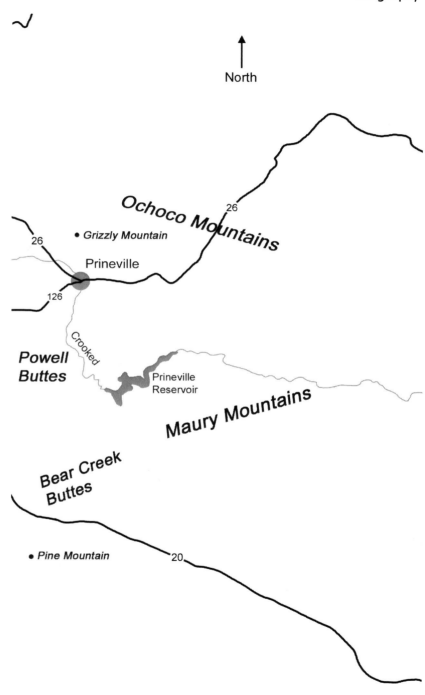

North

walled rimrock. All of this sits before the stunning volcanic backdrop of the Cascades.

Rivers and Lakes

Though this is an arid region, there are many rivers, creeks, and streams, thanks to snowmelt from the Cascades. Some creeks are fed directly from snow fields. Others are fed from springs as water percolates underground for miles through porous lava formations. All drain into our three main rivers:

- The Deschutes River originates in the Cascades just west of Mt. Bachelor, flows south to Wickiup Reservoir, then makes a U-turn north, flowing through Sunriver and Bend. This river is a major source of irrigation water for Central Oregon and is also popular for white water rafting.

- The Metolius River starts as a series of springs below Black Butte, a mountain northwest of Sisters. Because it is spring-fed, water temperatures and flows remain stable, making this scenic river world famous for year-round fishing.

- The Crooked River begins in the mountains east of Bend, flows through Prineville Reservoir, past Prineville, and wraps around Smith Rock.

All three rivers flow into Lake Billy Chinook, a man-made reser-

Springs feeding the Metolius River.

voir near Madras. The reservoir drains into a continuation of the Deschutes River which heads north to the Columbia River. A myth exists that north-flowing rivers are rare and unusual. In reality, rivers don't care about compass direction; they simply follow the topography downhill. The heading a river follows is simply a matter of chance. North-flowing rivers, such as the Deschutes (and the Nile), are as numerous and common as rivers that flow in other directions.

Topography

Since our rivers flow north, obviously the landscape tilts downhill towards the Columbia River. As you travel north on Highway 97, this tilt becomes obvious as you note the elevations of major towns along the route (see chart). Also notice that the plant communities change from forest in Sunriver to grassy plains in Madras. The higher elevations tend to be cooler and receive more rainfall.

Town	Elevation (feet)
Sunriver	4,185
Bend	3,625
Redmond	3,077
Madras	2,241

Mountains

Mountains give Central Oregon its unique character and stunning vistas. In future chapters you'll learn how our mountains affect the weather, creating dozens of different climates within the region. Mountains also influence rainfall and temperature, which in turn determine the plant communities and ecosystems of an area. Because of this interplay between mountains and climate, the region is comprised of a wonderful variety of wet and dry forests, grasslands, arid plains, and river canyons with hidden forests. It's impossible to get bored with the scenery here!

The best place for viewing mountains is from the top of Pilot Butte in Bend. If you want, your first field trip assignment could be to visit Pilot Butte and identify all the mountains in the area. The following photos, listing major peaks, were taken from this location.

Ochocos – This range, located northeast of Prineville, is a forested oasis in the middle of a parched region. One minute you are driving through sagebrush plains; the next, you find yourself in a towering ponderosa forest studded with flower-filled meadows and bubbling streams.

Newberry Volcano – To the south of Bend what appears to be a mountain range is actually a single, giant volcano. Look for the dozens of cinder cones dotting its flanks.

Cascade Mountains – Deep green forests give way to brilliant, white, symmetrical peaks providing a dramatic backdrop to Central Oregon. The entire range is volcanic, and while it looks peaceful now, these volcanoes are neither old nor extinct. The Cascades were named by settlers traveling the Oregon Trail. These pioneers had to navigate a series of notorious rapids on the Columbia River called "the Cascades." The mountains above the rapids were known as "the mountains by the Cascades" and the name evolved from there. Specific peaks in this range include:

- Mt. Jefferson, named by Lewis and Clark after their sponsor, Thomas Jefferson.

- Three Fingered Jack, Mt. Washington, and Broken Top. These used to be symmetrical, conical peaks but have been deeply eroded into their current unique shapes. They are no longer active volcanoes.

- The Three Sisters, originally named by Methodist ministers as Faith (north), Hope (middle), and Charity (south).

- Due to the success of the ski resort there, Bachelor Butte was renamed Mt. Bachelor by the Oregon Geographic Names Board. (I guess a marketing department thought skiers would rather ski a mountain instead of a butte.)

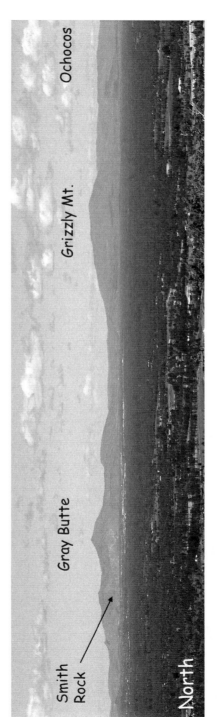

Smith Rock — Gray Butte — Grizzly Mt. — Ochocos

North

Powell Buttes — Maury Mts

East

11

Beyond Sagebrush

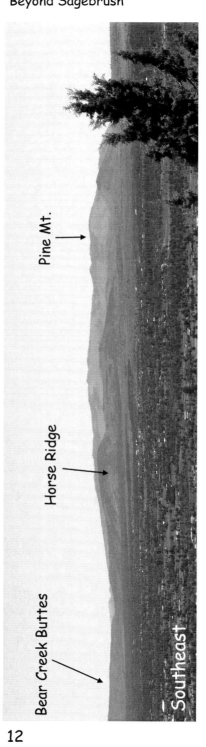

12

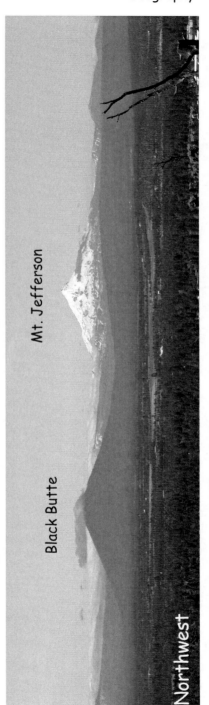

13

The High Desert

The word "desert" makes some people think of sand dunes, cactus, searing heat, and barren wastelands. But these are stereotypical images from movies. I've hiked the Mojave Desert and have seen few cacti; yet I've seen wild cactus in Hawaii. Some deserts are hot, but so are jungles; and the Gobi Desert is bitter cold. The Sahara has sand dunes, but so does the Oregon coast. So much for stereotypes!

As a child, I pictured a desert as dust, rock, and the occasional saguaro cactus. When I visited my first desert, on a trip to Nevada, I was surprised to see it covered with sagebrush, and not a cactus in sight. Since then, I've visited several deserts and now have a more accurate image of what a "typical" desert looks like: an arid, treeless area covered with widely spaced, low shrubs. Of course, deserts can also have trees, cacti, sand dunes, and salt flats. But if I

Opposite page: Typical high desert. Hmmm... doesn't look like a desert.

Stereotype desert. Typical American desert.

were to teleport you to a random location in an American desert, you would most likely see what I described.

Central Oregon is known as the "High Desert" to people in the Northwest. It's understood that elevation plays an important role in making this area unique, separating our area from the "Low Deserts" to the south. But what exactly is a "High Desert"?

What is a Desert?

Let's start by defining a desert. Surprisingly, scientists do not have an official, precise definition for the term, but most agree that it's a region in which:

- Less than ten inches of rain falls per year

- Evaporation is higher than precipitation (in other words, the air is very dry.)

The Great Deserts of North America

There are four great deserts in North America all of which are located in the American Southwest. Two deserts spread out into Northern Mexico. Each desert is distinctive and features plants unique to that area.

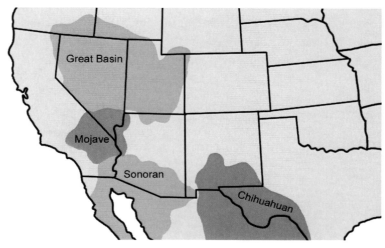

The four North American great deserts.

Chihuahuan Desert – This high elevation desert has hot summers and cool winters. Most rain comes from summer monsoons from the Gulf of Mexico. It is the home to Carlsbad Caverns and El Paso, Texas. Characteristic plants are agave and yucca.

Mojave Desert – Our smallest desert, the Mojave is home to Las Vegas, Edwards Air Force Base (a Space Shuttle landing site), and Death Valley (home to the lowest elevation in the United States at minus 282 feet and the hottest recorded temperature at 134 degrees.) It is hot, dry, windy, and known for Joshua trees.

Mojave Desert with Joshua trees.

17

Sonoran Desert – This is one of the hottest deserts in North America and home to the stereotypical Saguaro Cactus. It is unusual in that there are two rainy seasons and it has more plant diversity than more temperate regions. That busts the "barren desert" concept!

Sonoran Desert with Saguaro Cactus.

Great Basin – This is the largest and coldest desert in North America and is home to Reno, Salt Lake City, and the Great Salt Lake. It is called a basin because there are no outlets to the sea; rivers drain onto valley floors where the water simply evaporates, leaving behind salt flats (playas). Sagebrush is so common that the region has been described as an "ocean of sagebrush".

Great Basin—an ocean of sagebrush.

Is the High Desert a Desert?

Notice that the Oregon High Desert, which lies north of the Great Basin Desert, is not considered one of the great deserts of North America. Why not? Our climate is certainly arid, and Redmond, with nine inches of annual rainfall, fits the definition of a desert. But this region is more lush than a typical desert, with a lot more trees and grasses. Bend, with twelve inches of annual rainfall, is not a desert and supports large ponderosa forests. As you travel through the region, you'll see a patchwork of grasslands, sagebrush plains, woodlands, and forests – but no desert. What is going on here?

The Oregon High Desert is more accurately described as a shrub-steppe. If you arrange climate types in order of "wetness", from desert to rain forest, a steppe is the next climate up from a desert. While arid, there's enough water here to support plants that wouldn't normally be found in a true desert. Like the Great Basin, this region supports vast areas of sagebrush, but we also have vast grasslands and forests. So, while it certainly is an arid region, it's not arid enough to classify it as a great desert of North America.

Is the High Desert High?

The plains of Central Oregon are roughly 3,000 feet in elevation and the highest local mountain is Paulina Peak, close to 8,000 feet (This excludes the Cascades, which comprise a different climate region and ecosystem). That elevation certainly classifies this region as high, and it's definitely higher than communities in the Willamette Valley.

But compared to other deserts, the elevation in Central Oregon is unremarkable. Most of the Chihuahuan Desert is higher than 4,000 feet with peaks up to 10,000 feet. The Mojave averages 2,000-5,000 feet with peaks reaching 12,000 feet. The Great Basin averages over 4,000 feet with peaks over 14,000 feet. In fact the *only* desert lower than Central Oregon is the Sonoran, which is between sea level and 3,500 feet. For a supposedly "high" desert, we rank pretty low on the list.

"High Desert" in Bend.

What is a "High Desert"?

At what elevation does a region become a high desert and what's the significance of that elevation? These questions are impossible to answer because there is no definition for the term "high desert". Scientists don't use the term, and you won't find the High Desert listed on any maps. And, as I previously explained, this area (which is not a desert) is lower than most deserts in the United States.

So, if this place isn't the High Desert, what is it? This region is a part of the Columbia River Basin. It's the drainage basin for the Columbia River and encompasses Oregon, Washington, Idaho, and parts of Canada. As its name implies, all rivers in the basin drain into the Columbia River, then out to the Pacific. And, as mentioned earlier, the climate is shrub-steppe, not desert. A better name for the region would be "Central Oregon" since it at least refers to a geographic area found on a map.

Despite the name's lack of scientific significance, locals still refer to the area as the High Desert. And why not? After all, this region is higher than the Willamette Valley and arid as well, so "High Desert" certainly is a useful description. The name has an exciting, romantic quality, evoking images of sagebrush, sunny skies, and exotic mountainous landscapes, which is exactly what this place is all about!

Hot vs. Cold Deserts

Most people think deserts are hot, but this isn't always the case. It's true that deserts closer to the equator get toasty. If you've ever experienced 120 degree temperatures in Palm Springs, you'd know what I mean. But cold deserts exist. Examples include:

- The Great Basin

- The Gobi Desert in Northern China/Southern Mongolia

- The Atacama near the coasts of Peru and Chile

- And bizarrely, Antarctica (Low snowfall and dry air. Yes, it's a desert.)

These deserts are cold because they are farther north (or south) of the Equator. They receive less intense sunlight due to their latitude, so they don't heat up as much. They are deserts due to low rainfall and dry air, usually due to prevailing weather patterns or mountains that block rain storms.

In Central Oregon, it's common to see sagebrush plains covered in snow. But our snow is usually measured in inches and melts off quickly. We don't get the bitter cold and intense blizzards common on the East Coast. Still, as a cold region, we do have a shorter growing season than more temperate areas. But there's lots of good news, too. We often get sparkling clear winter days with plenty of sun. And even better, summers are fantastic. It's never miserably hot and there's no sweltering humidity. Yes, you'll experience the occasional day that hits 95 degrees in the afternoon, but it cools off pleasantly at night. (For comparison, I remember typical summer days in the Mojave where the temperature reached 95 degrees by 8:00 am and the coldest it ever got at night was 88 degrees! Yikes!)

Climate

Central Oregon has amazing and ever changing skies. Our wide open vistas give a clear view of weather patterns as clouds move in and out of the region. The sky changes quickly here; it looks different every hour. Other cities seem to have more consistent, slowly changing weather patterns. It's more exciting here. In addition to our restless skies, we experience booming thunderstorms, spooky dust devils, and bizarre flying saucer clouds. It rains, hails, and snows. Ice even forms out of thin air, coating trees with delicate crystals. I never paid much attention to the sky until I moved to Central Oregon. Now I'm enthralled.

Oregon – Not as Wet as You'd Think

Most people consider Oregon a wet and rainy state with gray skies and lush forests. But two thirds of the state is a dry, deserty plateau, filled with sagebrush and grasslands. And the western third of the

Opposite page: Cumulus clouds over Mt. Bachelor.

state is not as wet as people think. Portland gets about 43 inches of rain per year, which is much less than cities on the East Coast, and not too different from Dallas, Texas.

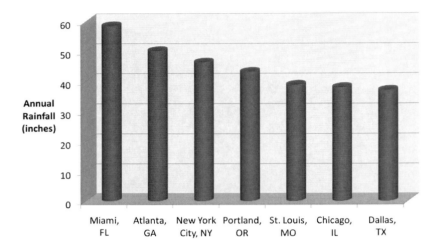

So, how did Oregon get its wet reputation? In most parts of the United States, it rains all year long, with most rain falling during brief but intense thunderstorms. This pattern results in a lot of sunny days, with occasional rainstorms. But in Western Oregon, particularly in the Willamette Valley, it drizzles almost constantly from October through June. Those many damp, drizzly, gray days create the impression of a waterlogged region. Our major cities, airports, and highways are in the western part of the state where most visitors travel, so that's what they see.

The mountain regions of Oregon, however, definitely earn a rainy reputation. Both the Coast Range and the Cascades are extremely wet, receiving enough precipitation to support temperate rain forests. The town of Cascade Locks, located 40 miles east of Portland in the heart of the Cascades, gets soaked with almost 80 inches of rain per year. Yet east of the Cascades, the remaining two thirds of the state, is arid steppe – not quite a desert, but a distinctly arid region. People unfamiliar with the Northwest may not know about this dry plateau.

Why Are the Mountains so Wet and the East so Dry?

Oregon's wet/dry split personality is due to the Cascade Mountains. How do they affect climate?

Moist air from the Pacific Ocean flows eastward over Oregon and is deflected upwards by the Cascade Mountains. As the air rises, it cools off and water condenses as rain. This is why Western Oregon and particularly, the western slopes of our mountain ranges, are so wet.

As the air mass reaches the crest of the Cascades, it blows over the top, and then follows the slopes down into the eastern part of the state. Two things are notable at this point. First, most of the moisture in the air is gone, having been dumped onto the mountains. Second, as the air descends, it starts to warm, so water stops condensing out as rain. The result is drier, sunnier weather and an arid climate in the eastern parts of Oregon.

You may notice that not all of eastern Oregon is dry. For example, Prineville has an arid climate and is surrounded by sagebrush. But a few miles to the east are the Ochoco Mountains, covered with forests, flower meadows, and streams. You've probably guessed the reason – as the air mass hits the mountains, it rises, cools, and moisture falls as rain. And, sure enough, to the east of these mountains, it's dry again. Also note that the Ochocos aren't as lush as the west-

Wet West.   Dry East.

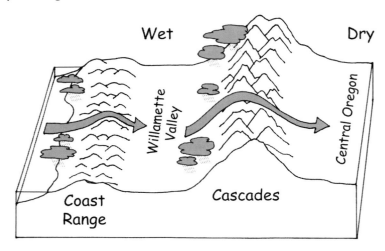

Wet · Dry · Willamette Valley · Central Oregon · Coast Range · Cascades

ern slopes of the Cascades. That's because most of the moisture fell on the Cascades, leaving much less water to be extracted when it reaches the Ochocos.

Climate of Central Oregon

If you're thinking of vacationing or relocating to Central Oregon, let's be honest – it's not a tropical paradise. For endless springtime, you need to go to San Diego or Hawaii (and pay the exorbitant cost of living). But if you take Central Oregon on its own terms, it can be quite pleasant. Winters get cold, but we don't experience the biting chill or paralyzing blizzards found in the eastern part of the United States. You can enjoy winter activities such as skiing, snow-mobiling, and snowshoeing without suffering. Our storms dump snow measured in inches, not feet, and it melts off rapidly.

Summers are perfect – it's never insufferably hot, there's no sticky humidity, and very little rain falls. It's ideal weather for biking, kayaking, golfing, camping, or hiking. Throughout the year there's plenty of sunshine. Storms are often followed by brilliantly blue, sunny skies, brightening your mood no matter what the season. You can enjoy four full seasons, and during winter, thanks to our conif-erous forests, the landscape remains pleasantly green. What are the factors that make this climate so unique?

It's dry — After releasing its moisture over the Cascades, air reaching Central Oregon is relatively dry. This results in less rain and more sunny days. For example, Bend averages twelve inches of rain per year, compared to the 43 inches Portland receives. Redmond is even drier with nine inches.

Dry air also has lower humidity, which makes for comfortable living. Summer days aren't sweaty and sticky. Winters are cold, but not bone-chilling. The air feels crisp and fresh.

Dry air makes for clear skies since there's no moisture blocking the view. During the day, the sky is a brilliant blue and you can see for miles. There's no haze and it rarely gets foggy. At night, the stars sparkle in an ebony sky.

It's not too hot... Central Oregon doesn't get extremely hot in the summer. Our latitude is such that the sun's rays strike the ground at an angle, reducing their intensity, unlike the blistering sunlight pounding the deserts further south. In Bend, the average temperature in July and August is 81 degrees. The all-time record high was 104 degrees. Compare this to Phoenix, where the average daily temperature in July is 105 degrees; one degree hotter than the hottest day ever in Bend!

...But it does get cold — Central Oregon is almost at the halfway point between the equator and North Pole, putting us close to arctic air masses. As high and low pressure systems come in off the Pacific Ocean, they rotate, pulling cold air down from the arctic and Canada. Sometimes a weather system results in frigid air over Canada being pulled through Idaho and Montana into the Columbia Basin. Central Oregon is surrounded by mountains on three sides, so this cold air is trapped here, creating our coldest weather. Such a weather pattern can also create freezing fog: water droplets freeze as rime ice on trees, turning them into delicate crystal sculptures.

The western side of the state is more temperate, even though it's at the same latitude as Central Oregon. Two factors help keep the west side warmer. First they are closer to the ocean, which has a moder-

Rime ice crystals forming on a tree.

ating effect on climate. Second, the Cascade Mountains block cold air masses coming down from Canada.

Temperatures in our region often drop below freezing. The average low in Bend during December and January is 23 degrees. It's not unusual to see sagebrush plains covered in snow. The growing season is short, lasting from May through September, and our coldest months are January and February. The snow season is very unpredictable and is influenced heavily by El Niño and La Niña weather events. We get heavy snow years, light snow years, years where the only snow falls early (or late) in the season, and there are even times when snow falls on the Fourth of July! You just never know, so keep that snow shovel handy!

Temperatures swing wildly — Humid air and bodies of water absorb heat during the day, then release it at night. Clouds form an insulating blanket over land, holding warmth in at night. Because of these effects, coastal towns enjoy mild climates; the difference between daytime highs and nighttime lows is only 10-15 degrees. In Central Oregon, temperatures can swing 40 degrees in one day. On a summer day, it's typical for a 95 degree day to be followed by a 58 degree night – perfect for cooling off your house.

The charts compare Bend to the coastal town of Florence, which is directly to the west and at the same latitude. Notice that Florence has milder temperatures and less difference between the daily high and low temperatures.

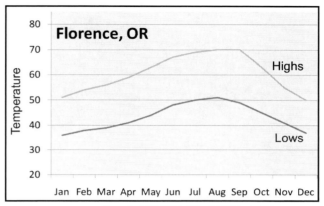

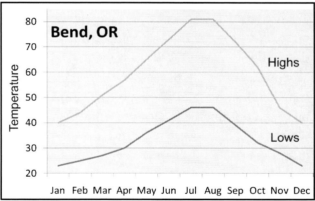

Most precipitation is in the form of snow — Most of the rivers and lakes in Central Oregon are fed by snowmelt from the mountains. The Columbia Plateau receives enough snow to support year-round rivers such as the Deschutes. The continuous flow of these rivers supports a lush, riparian ecosystem along their banks. These riverbanks are like a lush oasis in an otherwise dry region.

A variety of climates — In general, Central Oregon has a cool, arid climate. Yet Bend receives more rain than Redmond. Madras is located in a dry, grassy plain and Sunriver is in forest. Ski resorts are built on the north sides of mountains because the snow is deeper

A beautiful snowy day in Bend

and lasts longer. These local variations in weather are called micro-climates.

Terrain has a big effect on climate and even small mountains can affect the weather. For example, Awbrey Butte in Bend is mostly dry, juniper forest. But the north side gets slightly more moisture, so a pocket of ponderosa grows there. It can be raining in Bend, but snowing on the top of the butte. Our terrain is so varied that about one hundred microclimates are known to exist in the region. In Central Oregon, it's not unusual for two places a mile apart to have different weather, a fact that would amaze someone who lives east of the Rockies.

Sunlight Seasons

As a person who grew up in a lower latitude, I find the long summer days in Central Oregon unusual. At 9:00 p.m., it's still bright outside and twilight seems to last forever (great for evening patio parties). Even when the skies finally turn black and the stars come out, there's still a faint blue glow on the northern horizon. Further south, the sun seems to be in a hurry, setting before 8:00 p.m. with a short twilight. What causes these differences in light patterns?

As you know, the days are long in summer and short in winter. That's because the earth is tilted to one side as it orbits the sun. When the earth is on one side of its orbit, the northern hemisphere is tilted towards the sun. Sunlight hits at a more direct angle and illuminates more of the upper globe. This is why the North Pole has 24 hours of daylight on the longest day of the year.

Six months later, the earth is orbiting the other side of the sun, so the northern hemisphere is tilted away. Sunlight hits at such a low angle that the North Pole experiences no daylight during the shortest day of winter.

Day length changes depending on how close you are to the poles. Day length is pretty consistent close to the equator. For example, in Hawaii the days and nights are roughly equal in length all year round. But as you continue north, summer days get longer and winter days get shorter.

On the longest day of the year, Bend receives about one hour more sunlight than Los Angeles, 800 miles to the south. In Los Angeles, it becomes dark soon after sunset, while in Bend, twilight lingers, making the day seem even longer.

On the shortest day of winter, the situation is reversed. Los Angeles receives one more hour of daylight than Bend. Also, the sun appears much higher in the sky, so it seems brighter. In Bend, sunlight hits the earth at a greater angle and the sun appears lower in the sky. Because of the angle, sunlight must travel through more atmos-

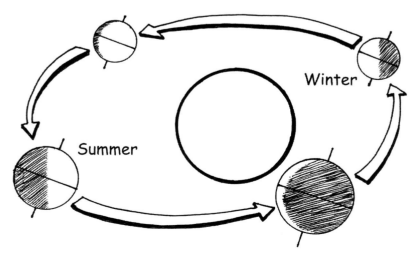

phere. The air molecules scatter blue and violet tones, giving our winter sunlight a yellow tinge. It feels like sunset at 2 p.m.

Clouds

It's rare to see a monotonous, gray, overcast layer in Central Oregon. Instead, the sky is usually a riot of puffy clouds, wispy threads, layers, and sheets. Sunsets on days with clouds are spectacular; the sky afire with color.

What is a cloud? It's simply a fog of tiny water droplets (or ice if the cloud is cold enough). As air cools, its ability to hold moisture drops and water condenses out as fog.

Types of Clouds

Central Oregon is great for cloud watching. The sky changes constantly and is different every hour. It's easy to identify clouds and each type tells a different story:

Cirrus — These are thin, wispy, and almost transparent. They are made from ice crystals and are found at high altitudes. If they start to thicken or become prominent, they are usually the precursor of bad weather, indicating an approaching front. If they stay thin and wispy, the weather will probably be clear and stable.

Cumulus — These look like mounds of cotton candy. They are the classic, stereotypical shape that comes to mind when people visualize a cloud. While they can be associated with bad weather, they also appear in the afternoons on fine summer days and don't necessarily mean you should cancel your picnic.

Stratus — These are flat gray sheets that cover the sky and block the sun. When present, you can expect rain or snow.

Bizarre clouds — Contrails, produced by aircraft, are man-made clouds. Whenever fuel burns, water is created as a byproduct. You can see this on the ground - on a cold morning, notice the water dripping out of a car's exhaust pipe. High up in the atmosphere this water condenses into ice crystals, leaving an arrow-straight cloud behind an airplane. If there are winds aloft, the contrail spreads into a wide ribbon.

Lenticular clouds are often found over the mountains in Central Oregon. These fascinating formations look like a lens or even a flying saucer. They are formed when strong winds blowing from the west hit the volcanoes of the Cascades at a perpendicular angle. The wind rises until it reaches the peak, then flows downhill on the other side. This sets up an oscillation pattern downwind from the mountain; wind continues to rise and fall, despite the fact that there is no longer a mountain peak to direct the air. This pattern can continue up to 100 miles downwind from the peak.

Contrail.   Lenticular cloud.

As the air rises, it cools, forming a cloud. But at the same level on
the other side, the cloud dissipates as the downward moving air
warms. The result appears as a "lens" or "cap" sitting on the mountain peak. Despite the fact that the cloud appears stationary, its
streamlined shape indicates that the winds are blowing fast. The
cloud is forming rapidly on one side and dissipating just as fast on
the other. Since these winds flow in layers, you may see several
"hats" sitting one on top of the other above the peak. And remember that oscillation downwind from the peak? Lens shaped clouds
can form at the peaks of each oscillation. So don't be surprised to
see "flying saucers" over Bend and Redmond.

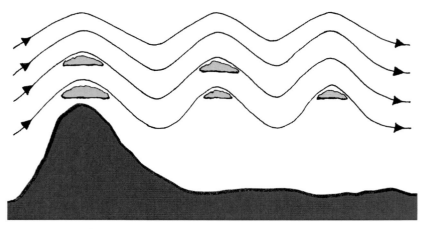

Wind oscillations creating lens clouds.

Precipitation

When conditions are right, water falls out of clouds in the form of precipitation. In general, a cloud is simply a collection of microscopic water droplets or ice crystals that have condensed out of the air. They are so small that the resistance of air is enough to keep them floating in the sky. But if they get large enough, gravity takes over and they fall as precipitation.

Precipitation takes many forms:

Rain — If a water droplet grows large enough it simply falls out of the sky. This can happen in three ways. First, the water droplet can grow as water continues to condense out of the air. Or water droplets can collide and combine with other droplets until they get heavy enough to fall. The last process is a bit more complicated. The cloud can be so cold that ice crystals and super-cooled water droplets exist side by side. As the water droplets evaporate, their moisture condenses on the ice crystals, causing them to grow. When the crystals get heavy enough they fall and melt on the way down.

Sometimes rain falls out of a cloud but evaporates before it hits the ground. This results in a cloud layer with streaks of rain that seem to hang in the air. This phenomenon is called virga and is a common sight in Central Oregon.

Virga

Snow — Snow is created when moisture condenses directly onto a particle, usually dust, and forms an ice crystal. As the crystal grows, it gets heavy enough to fall. It snows often in Central Oregon, but typically, only a few inches accumulate. However, we do get winters with above average snowfall. Over the winter of

1973-74 a record 90.6 inches of snow fell on Bend (normally Bend gets about 32 inches of snow per year.)

Ice crystals falling from cirrus clouds create wispy plumes called fall streaks. Like virga, this snow evaporates soon after leaving the cloud.

Jeff Lowe

Fall streaks.

Ice pellets and hail — Sometimes freezing air exists below a rain cloud. As water droplets fall through this layer, they freeze into pellets; or the pellets can combine to form hail. Our hailstorms can be severe. In July of 2006, a freak storm dumped golf ball-sized hail for twelve minutes on the area around the Bend airport. Unfortunately, a local aircraft manufacturer had over sixty new planes out on the tarmac, which were damaged. Witnesses saw hail hitting the ground and bouncing up to ten feet into the air.

Thermals

On summer days in Central Oregon, it's common to see a sky filled with puffy white clouds called "fair weather cumulus." The morning starts out sunny and warm with a clear sky. As the day progresses, the sky fills with these puffy white clouds, despite the fact that no rain is forecast. Then, as evening falls, the clouds disappear. What causes this strange weather?

On summer days, the sun heats the ground, which in turn heats the air directly above it. A bubble of warm air forms and rises into the sky. Warm air is less dense than cool air, so it has a tendency to rise. (That's what makes hot-air balloons float.) This bubble of

Fair weather cumulus clouds. No rain today!

warm air is called a thermal. If you could see this process taking place, it would look like the blobs of oil rising in a lava lamp.

When a bubble rises far enough, the air cools, water condenses, and a cloud forms. The cloud is a puffy, white cumulus cloud with a flat base. Water droplets on its top and edges will evaporate, cooling the air. This cool air falls back to the ground. The downward flow prevents other clouds from forming nearby, so the cloud is isolated in the sky, surrounded by clear air. The cloud will last until the thermal dissipates, usually from five to forty-five minutes.

You can't see thermals but you can see the puffy clouds they form.

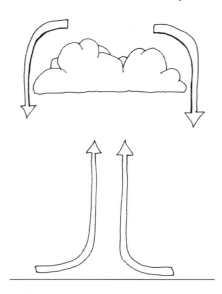

Thermal

Remember that this process is happening over hundreds of square miles, resulting in a sky filled with evenly spaced clouds, each one surrounded by an area of clear space.

Travelers flying into Central Oregon during the summer know that these thermals create bumpy air. Below the cloud, a bubble of warm air is rising and cool air is falling around the perimeter. This creates turbulence that can be felt as soon as the airplane descends below the cloud deck. The plane is flying through bumpy air and is similar to a boat sailing across choppy water. It's nothing to worry about and is more annoying than dangerous.

Dust Devils

Dust devils are spinning columns of air similar to tornadoes. Tornadoes, however, are much stronger and are generated by thunderstorms. Dust devils, surprisingly, are caused by beautiful, warm, sunny days. They can be seen throughout Central Oregon during the summer. From a distance, you'll see a column of dust rising gently into the air; you may think it's just a car driving on a dirt road. But up close, dust devils can be unsettling. Seemingly out of nowhere a surprisingly violent vortex appears and dances across the landscape as if guided by some unearthly intelligence. Then abruptly, it disappears.

A dust devil begins as a thermal, a blob of hot air rising into the sky. Under the correct conditions, the blob stretches out and begins to spin. Nearby hot air is sucked into the bottom of the vortex and rises, intensifying the spin. If the ground is dusty, dirt is sucked into the vortex as well, making the airflow visible. The spinning effect creates a forward momentum and dust devils usually travel across the landscape. Most dust devils are less than three feet in diameter, with winds blowing up to forty-five miles per hour. They last a few minutes, then dissipate suddenly as the warm air is exhausted.

Dust devil.

Several factors contribute to the formation of a dust devil. First, the weather must be sunny with clear skies. This allows the sun to heat the ground, creating pockets of warm air which rise as thermals. Second, flat and relatively barren terrain increases the likelihood that enough hot air will be produced to "fuel" the vortex. The barren terrain has exposed soil, providing the dust that makes the dust devil visible. Our soils in Central Oregon are particularly dusty, resulting in dust devils that are especially visible. Finally, the air must be cool with no wind. The difference in temperature between the hot surface of the ground and the cooler upper air powers the dust devil. On a windy day the warm and cool air mix, eliminating this differential. Once you understand the conditions that create dust devils, you'll know where and when to look for them. They are common on the flat plains around Bend and Redmond.

Compared to a tornado, dust devils are not very powerful. The strongest dust devils, which are rare, grow to three hundred feet in diameter with winds up to seventy-five miles per hour, which puts them in the same category as a weak tornado. But even an average dust devil can knock you around. If you see a dust devil crossing the road in front of your car, slow down. The winds can batter your vehicle and even blow you off the road. For the same reason, the control tower at the Redmond airport keeps a watch for dust devils in order to warn pilots.

Thunderstorms

Residents of Central Oregon have the privilege of experiencing spectacular thunderstorms during the summer. These storms feature huge dark clouds, intense downpours, booming thunder, sudden blasts of wind, and breathtaking lighting streaking across the sky. I love to watch thunderstorms, so during the summer, I keep an eye on the sky and internet radar maps. If a thunderstorm cell is approaching my house, I find a good viewing window to watch the show. Thunderstorms are spectacular, different every time, and free!

Three conditions must be met before a thunderstorm can form; all of them are prevalent in Central Oregon:

Unstable air – Usually caused by a weather pattern that moves cooler air into the upper atmosphere.

Thunderstorm building over Newberry Volcano.

A lifting force - Winds blowing across the landscape hit mountains and are directed upwards. In Central Oregon, you may notice that thunderstorms tend to form over Newberry Volcano, the Cascades, and the Ochocos.

Moisture – Our moisture flows in from the Pacific. The most powerful thunderstorms are created when swirling air around a low pressure system pumps moist air through Southern Oregon, over Klamath Falls and up into Central Oregon.

You might think such powerful and wet storms would be prevalent on the rainy, western side of the state, but thunderstorms are actually more common on the drier, eastern side. There are several reasons for this. The west does not have the geography to create strong uplifting forces. The air is cooler and more stable. Finally, the factors that make the western climate mild and temperate are not conducive to thunderstorms. The west side is more likely to get gentle storms with rain falling from stratus clouds.

The Stages of a Thunderstorm

Thunderstorms progress through three observable stages. Start by watching weather forecasts and look for predictions of thunderstorm activity. The day usually starts out sunny and hot, with spectacular blue, cloudless skies. By noon, fair weather cumulus clouds will appear, seemingly out of nowhere. As the day progresses, the clouds will grow quickly until they look like monstrous mounds of cotton.

During the first, or cumulus, stage of a thunderstorm, a cumulus cloud begins to grow vertically. A lifting force, usually winds deflected upward by mountains, pushes warm air into the cooler atmosphere. The moisture in the air condenses, creating water droplets and releasing heat. The heat rises, creating further uplift. Water droplets get caught in this wind and are trapped in a cycle of rising and falling, growing larger as more water condenses out of the air. This creates an ever-building cycle in which water condenses, releasing heat, which intensifies the uplift.

During this stage, the clouds grow rapidly, towering into the sky as far as 20,000 feet and expanding to three to five miles in diameter. The words "growing rapidly" are significant; these clouds grow as much as fifteen feet per second, and seem to double in size every time you glance at the sky! These towering cumulus clouds indicate the cumulus stage of a thunderstorm.

During the second, or mature stage of a thunderstorm, water drops grow in size, becoming heavy enough to resist the uplifting winds and start falling to the ground. This is the most intense stage of a thunderstorm; as the droplets fall on one side of the cloud, warm air is rising up to 150 miles per hour on the other side, fueling the cy-

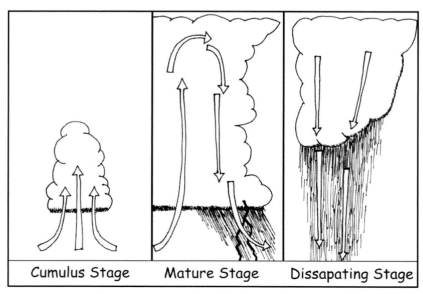

| Cumulus Stage | Mature Stage | Dissapating Stage |

cle. On the ground, you will experience torrential rains, hail, high winds, thunder, lighting, and blasts of surprisingly cold air as it rushes down from the top of the cloud.

By this time the cloud tops have reached high into the atmosphere, as much as 40,000 feet. At this altitude, the lifting motion within the cloud is weak and high winds at that level shear the tops of the clouds into the classic anvil shape of thunderheads. The point of the anvil stretches downwind and literally points in the direction the storm is headed.

The dissipating stage signals the end of a thunderstorm. At this point, so much cold air and water is falling out of the cloud that the updraft is disrupted. The heat and moisture needed to drive the storm is now cut off and the storm gradually weakens. The clouds start to dissipate, and by sunset, the skies may be clear again.

Lightning

Lighting is a static discharge, much like the tiny shock you receive after walking across a carpet and touching a doorknob – but far more powerful. While not fully understood by scientists, the static buildup seems to be created by falling water droplets and colliding ice crystals, which create areas of positive and negative potential. When the potential builds up high enough, a spark jumps between the positive and negatively charged areas.

A thousand foot lightning bolt can generate a billion volts. This energy ionizes the air, releasing light and heating the air to 18,000 degrees Fahrenheit in an instant. This rapid heating creates a pressure wave heard as thunder.

Observing Thunderstorms

How can you predict the path of the thunderstorm? You have probably heard of the Boy Scout technique of watching for a flash and counting the seconds until you hear a boom of thunder. Sound travels one mile in five seconds, so divide the number of seconds by five to get the distance to the lighting flash. (For example, if you count ten seconds between the lighting and the thunder, the lighting is two miles away) However, there are easier methods of predicting the path of a thunderstorm:

- Thunderstorms move fast. If you have a good vantage point, simply watch where the wall of rain is moving.

- Count the number of seconds between a lighting flash and the thunder. If this interval gets shorter, the storm is coming toward you. If it is getting longer, the storm is moving away.

- Go to www.weather.com and watch the Doppler radar image, which updates every five minutes. You can run the animation and watch storms move across your area. A thunder cell is easy to identify – it will be a blob of yellow or red (indicating intense rainfall). You will probably notice several thunder cells moving across the area.

Thunderstorms can be dangerous because of lighting, winds, and hail. When thunderstorms are predicted, don't plan an afternoon hike to a mountain peak. Instead, wait for another day. Thunderstorms build fast, so if you see serious cloud buildup while hiking, do not assume you have time to reach the peak. Turn around immediately.

Climate Trivia

Tornadoes are extremely rare in Central Oregon.

Inland fog is the hardest weather condition to forecast.

The largest hailstone ever found weighed 1.6 pounds. It was the size of a Nerf football. The largest hailstone seen by a local forecaster in Central Oregon was golf-ball sized.

Geology

The geology of Central Oregon can be summarized in one word: volcanoes! What is more exciting than an erupting volcano? The volcanoes of Central Oregon seem peaceful and serene today but these mountains are just as active now as they were in the past. They are neither old nor extinct. Mt. St. Helens erupted in 1980 and Mt. Lassen erupted in 1914. Eight Cascade peaks erupted during the 1800's. As for local volcanoes, Newberry last erupted 1,300 years ago, which is equivalent to yesterday on a geologic timescale. This mountain is literally "hot," with magma so close to the surface that Newberry is being considered as a source of geothermal power production.

Fortunately there's no need to cancel your vacation plans. On a human timescale, these eruptions are spaced apart by decades, many are small, and geologists can give us plenty of warning about impending eruptions.

Opposite page: Mt. Jefferson is a stratovolcano.

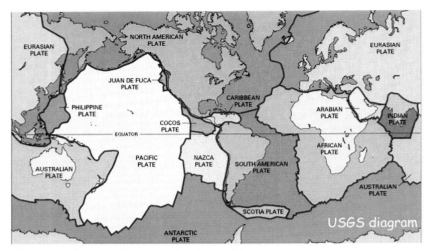

Plates that make up the Earth's crust.

How Oregon's Volcanoes Formed

Why are there volcanoes in Oregon? To understand, we need to start by looking at geology from a global perspective. The earth is a ball of molten rock (magma) covered in a thin crust, roughly three to thirty miles deep. It is so thin that if you could shrink the earth to the size of an apple, the crust would be as thick as the apple skin. Because it is so thin, the crust has cracked into a jigsaw puzzle of pieces, called plates, that literally float on the molten magma.

Things that float also move, and the earth's plates are slowly moving. Off the coasts of Oregon and Washington is a small plate called Juan de Fuca, sandwiched between the Pacific and North American Plates. Geologic forces are pushing this plate into North America, and as it collides with our continent, it's forced downwards into the earth. The edge of the plate melts due to friction and pressure; as a result, blobs of magma push up to the surface and erupt as volcanoes. The result is a region consisting of thousands of volcanoes stretching from Northern California to the Canadian border. Most are extinct, but as long as the Juan de Fuca plate keeps diving under the continent, eruptions will continue, as demonstrated by Mt. St. Helens.

A Brief Geologic History of Oregon

Warm Seas

(70 million years ago)

The western parts of Oregon and Washington were covered by a shallow, warm sea. Imagine it as a large bay opening to the Pacific Ocean. Bend would have been underwater and Pendleton would have been near the coast.

Volcanoes Erupt

(60-40 million years ago)

The Juan de Fuca plate began colliding with North America. The heavier ocean crust dove into the earth's interior as the lighter continent scraped over the top. Seafloor mud and rock were scraped onto the continent, building up the coastal range.

Meanwhile, about one hundred miles inland, the Cascade Mountains began to form. The leading edge of the Juan de Fuca plate melted as it dove, forming magma. The magma rose to the surface, creating volcanoes as it erupted onto the landscape. There were

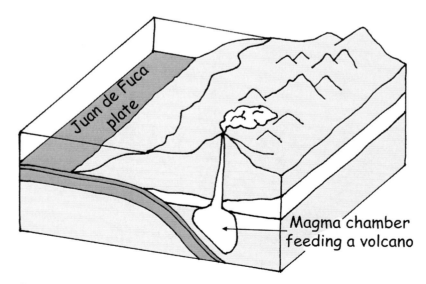

Magma chamber feeding a volcano

The Juan de Fuca plate moving under Oregon.

thousands of these eruptions, each layering a new mountain atop the previous volcano. The range developed into a jumble of volcanoes piled on top of each other. It's like a giant ice cream sundae made from thousands of scoops. During this time, the sea filled in, moving the Oregon coast westward to its current location.

Lava Floods

(17-12 million years ago)

Mysteriously, the Cascades volcanoes stopped erupting and all volcanic activity moved eastward. Along the Idaho border, in easternmost Oregon and Washington, a bizarre type of volcano began erupting. Unlike a normal volcano that belches ash, lava, or cinders, this was simply a crack in the earth's crust that poured out huge amounts of an extremely fluid lava. These cracks were a few dozen yards wide and hundreds of miles long. Because the lava was so thin, it spread over the landscape like a flood, which is why these flows are called flood basalts.

Hundreds of these volcanoes erupted, many disgorging more than one hundred cubic miles of lava, which flowed to cover thousands of square miles of land. As these eruptions progressed, the Northwest gradually became covered by lava, layer upon layer, to a depth of up to six thousand feet. Valleys were inundated. Hills were buried, with only the highest peaks sticking out of the lava plain. Mighty rivers, such as the Columbia, were forced into new channels. This was one of the largest basalt floods on earth, covering

Basalt columns near Smith Rock.

over 63,000 square miles.

The lava cooled to form a dark grey rock called basalt. As it cools, basalt cracks at 120 degree angles, creating vertical six-sided columns. These columns become visible when the landscape is eroded away by rivers. You can see basalt columns on cliffs around Lake Billy Chinook or on any steep river gorge in Central Oregon. A good place to see them is along Highway 26 as it dives down to the town of Warm Springs northwest of Madras. Such cliffs are known as rimrock.

Uplift

(12-4 million years ago)

The flood basalt eruptions were so prolific that magma chambers below the earth's crust drained. As a result, the landscape in the Columbia Basin gradually began to sink. Forces caused the landscape to tilt and mountains began to rise in the eastern part of the state. During this time the land rose along a slope starting at Smith Rock near Redmond to the Wallowa Mountains in the northeast. This uplift formed the Blue and Ochoco Mountains.

Majestic Peaks

(1 million years ago to present)

The Cascades stretched from Northern California to the Canadian border. They averaged 40-50 miles in width and 4,500 to 5,000 feet in elevation.

One million years ago, a second mountain range began to grow a few miles east of and parallel to the original Cascades. It formed the same way as the original Cascades did, from erupting volcanoes building mountains upon mountains. This process resulted in the stunning, symmetrical peaks of the High Cascades. These spectacular volcanoes include Mt. Hood, Mt. Jefferson, the Three Sisters, and Mt. Bachelor, all of which tower nine to eleven thousand feet into the sky, dwarfing the surrounding peaks.

When people think of a "typical" volcano, a stratovolcano (also

South Sister, a classic stratovolcano.

called "composite volcano") comes to mind. No wonder - these dramatic-looking peaks make up sixty percent of the volcanoes in the world. They are steep sided, conical peaks and can erupt violently. As the name implies, a stratovolcano is comprised of strata, or layers, of material. During an eruption, this material is deposited on the sides of the mountain. It could be chunky ash, cinders, or rock, or it could be gooey lava. Different eruptions deposit different layers; if you could cut a stratovolcano in half, its cross-section would look like a seven-layer Mexican dip (without the guacamole of course.)

Many volcanoes ejected ash clouds (as did Mt. St. Helens during its 1980 eruption). Volcanic ash is simply rock, pulverized into dust from violent explosions, and blown into the sky. The ash rained down upon the landscape of Central Oregon, helping to build up soils. The last major ash contribution occurred 7,700 years ago when Mt. Mazama exploded, forming Crater Lake.

Glaciers

(1.5 million years ago - present)

The current ice age began more than one million years ago and has cycled between eight cold and warm periods. We are still in this ice age, but obviously are in a warm period. During a cold cycle, snow builds up, packs into ice, and forms glacier sheets thousands of feet thick that cover the continent. The volcanic peaks of the Cascades would have been buried in this ice. Perhaps only the upper peaks would have poked above the ice sheet, but otherwise, there would have been no indication that there was a mountain range encased below. If a buried volcano erupted, it would simply blow through the hundreds of feet of ice above it.

The last cold event occurred between 100,000 and 12,000 years ago when ice formed a layer two thousand feet thick along the crest of the Cascades. These glaciers reached within seven miles of Bend. As the glaciers grew, gravity slowly dragged them downhill, scouring the mountainsides, creating deep canyons and bowls.

Several local peaks such as Broken Top, Mt. Washington, Three Fingered Jack, and Mt. Jefferson have been sculpted by glaciers, resulting in their current jagged appearance.

What's in Store for the Future?

Understanding geologic history is not like reading a book in which events are neatly wrapped up in the last chapter. Geologic history is a continuum of events, and there is no last chapter. The "book" never ends because new chapters are constantly being "written". Currently we are still in the stratovolcano phase that started one million years ago.

Broken Top, sculpted by glaciers.

Will an eruption happen in your lifetime? Certainly! It's extremely likely that a volcano will blow somewhere in the Cascades within the next few decades. Likely candidates are Mt. Shasta, Mt. Hood, Mt. Rainier, and Mt. Baker. The following local volcanoes are being watched by the US Geological Service:

Newberry Volcano – Any type of eruption is possible, from an oozing lava flow to a big KA-BOOM. These eruptions won't necessarily be centered on the crater; cinder cones could erupt on the flanks of the mountain.

Mt. Bachelor – An eruption is possible but unlikely. If it did erupt, it would possibly ooze slow moving lava. The lava would melt snow, creating mudflows and flooding (a bummer if you are skiing).

South Sister - About three miles west of South Sister there is a 100 -square-mile area of ground bulging upward. It's rising at the rate of one inch per year but has slowed recently. Geologists think it is caused by a lake of magma pooling almost five miles underground. Right now geologists can only speculate about what will happen, but if this activity causes an eruption, it would probably result in a cinder cone or lava flow.

Middle Sister – Not much is known about this peak, but geologists suspect that Middle Sister is as active as South Sister.

The rest of the volcanoes in the area – Broken Top, North Sister, Mt. Washington, Black Butte, Three Fingered Jack, and Mt. Jefferson – are probably extinct. But it is very likely that cinder cones could erupt anywhere along the Cascades.

Geologic Sites in the Region

Central Oregon is unique in that we have an unusually large variety of interesting geological features concentrated in our area. These places are fascinating to visit, accessible most of the year, and are close by. Directions to many of these features are listed in the Appendix. Here's a sampling:

The yellow and purple walls of Smith Rock tell an amazing story about a unique volcano.

Smith Rock

Just north of Redmond is a formation of jagged yellow and purple walls and towering spires. This heavily eroded area is Smith Rock State Park, a popular rock climbing destination. For many years prevailing geologic theory held that Smith Rock was the eroded remains of a small volcano known as a tuff cone. But recently, geologists have uncovered new evidence that this area was part of something big. Something very big. They now think Smith Rock is part of a supervolcano called the Crooked River Caldera, the largest volcano in Oregon.

The term "supervolcano" is not an official geologic term, but it's a handy way to describe the most enormous and powerful volcanoes on the planet. These volcanoes are so powerful that their eruptions alter global climate for years and can devastate the landscape for hundreds of miles.

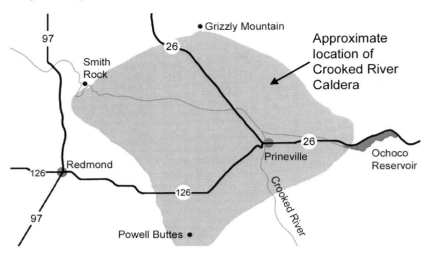

The Crooked River Caldera is the mouth of a huge volcano.

Roughly 29 million years ago, a supervolcano near Prineville erupted in a single, massive explosion. As the magma chamber under the volcano emptied, the volcano collapsed, producing a caldera about twenty miles in diameter. Ash from the eruption fell down, filling the caldera, and then fused together to form a yellow rock called welded tuff.

After the eruption, magma continued to push upward, producing smaller eruptions of rhyolite lava. The magma also circulated heat and hot fluids to the surface. These fluids rose along cracks at the edge of the caldera and reacted with the tuff, altering it chemically. The result was "tougher" tuff, able to resist erosion. There is also evidence that these fluids may have formed geysers and mud pots near Smith Rock, similar to those at Yellowstone.

Within the last million years or so, lava from the newly erupting Newberry Volcano flowed north and butted against Smith Rock. The current parking lot is built upon this lava flow and as you hike into the park, you can see the dark grey rocks of this formation. The lava forced the Crooked River to flow next to Smith Rock, cutting into the tuff. Eventually topsoil eroded away, exposing the harder tuff spires you see today.

There are probably more "Smith Rocks" out there, since the tuff fills the entire caldera. But most of it is buried under millions of years of lava flows, debris, and sediments. Currently we can only see the one formation. The chemically altered tuff is a stable rock that is great for rock climbing. Steep-sided walls rising 600 feet into the air add to the challenge. You'll also notice large reddish-purple formations, which are the rhyolite lavas that poured out following the main explosion.

Fort Rock Lake

This lake has no marinas, fishing access, or beaches. That's not surprising, since it hasn't held water for thousands of years! Today, the ancient lake bed is a vast desert plain, carpeted with sagebrush, rabbitbrush, and agricultural fields. Visit in late August, when blooms of rabbitbrush paint the desert floor a brilliant yellow.

Fort Rock Lake was one of eight, large pluvial lakes that formed in eastern Oregon during the last ice age. A pluvial lake is fed from rainwater and changes size during wet or dry spells. Tens of thousands of years ago, the climate in Central Oregon was cooler and wetter, with enough rain to form these lakes. Eventually the climate

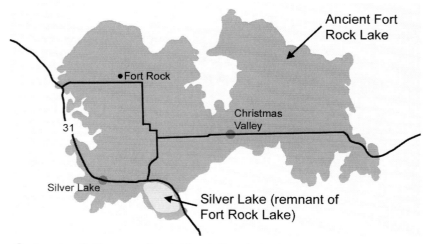

Extent of the ancient Fort Rock Lake.

changed, the weather became drier, and the lakes shrank away. In the case of Fort Rock Lake, all that remains is Silver Lake. Summer, Malheur, and Goose Lakes are the remnants of other pluvial lakes.

Fort Rock Lake filled the valley where its namesake is located. It extended east, past the town of Christmas Valley. At its maximum size 23,000 years ago, the lake covered 1,500 square miles and was 250 feet deep. At Fort Rock, the lake was about 150 feet deep. But when global warming happened over ten thousand years ago, the lake dried up, leaving the vast, flat valley you see today.

Hole in the Ground

A mysterious formation lies hidden in the forest just one and a half miles from Highway 31. Amid an open pine forest carpeted with sagebrush lies a beautifully symmetrical crater roughly a mile in diameter and 310 feet deep. At first glance, it looks like a meteor crater; but like most features in Oregon, it is actually volcanic.

Hole in the Ground is a maar crater created from a unique volcanic eruption. Sometime around one hundred thousand years ago, a blob of hot magma flowed upward along a fault line near the shore of Fort Rock Lake. The magma eventually rose to a level where the ground was saturated with lake water, roughly 1,000 to 1,600 feet

While it looks like a meteor crater, Hole in the Ground is a volcano.

Ft. Rock rising dramatically from the desert floor.

below the surface. The incredible heat from the magma flashed water into steam, creating a massive explosion. This explosion was so powerful, it threw chunks of rock up to twenty-six feet in diameter over two miles from the vent. After the initial explosion, the sides of the crater slumped to the center, plugging the vent. Water seeped back and restored the water table, priming the system for another explosion.

Over a period of days or weeks, magma continued to rise, creating new explosions. Eventually, a colossal crater roughly a mile in diameter formed. Over time, the sides slumped inward again, forming a smooth, symmetrical bowl similar to a meteor crater.

Hole in the Ground is quite large for a maar. Its symmetry is beautiful and awe-inspiring. The gently sloping sides and lack of vegetation make it easy to explore on foot, so you can hike right to the center of the eruption site.

Fort Rock

Rising 200 feet from the desert floor is the imposing Fort Rock. Its location on a flat desert plain and its vertical walls give this formation a fortress-like appearance.

Fort Rock has a lot in common with Hole in the Ground because it formed in a similar way. Rising magma encountered the wet mud at the bottom of Fort Rock Lake sometime between 50,000 and 100,000 years ago. The resulting steam explosion blew lava hundreds of feet into the air, creating a frothy ash, which fell in a ring around the volcanic vent. If you had been boating on the lake at that time, you would have seen what looked like a huge geyser as water, steam, and ash blew into the sky. Eventually, a ring-shaped island formed in the lake as the ash hardened into a rock called tuff. Fort Rock is the largest of over forty formations in this valley, all created in a similar manner.

Time passed and lake levels rose and fell. Wave action eroded terraces and benches, sculpting the outer walls. You can still see these wave marks today. The wave action wasn't consistent; due to prevailing southerly winds, the south side of the tuff ring was exposed to stronger wave action which gradually eroded the southern wall. It eventually collapsed, turning the ring into a shape resembling the letter "C".

Erosion from wave action.

When you visit Fort Rock, imagine what it was like here thousands of years ago. The parking lot would have been 150 feet underwater. Hike up to the crater floor, which is thirty feet higher than the surrounding desert. Thousands of years ago you would still be standing under water at the bottom of a cove surrounded by the protective rim of the crater. Looking up at the walls, you'll see erosion marks where waves pounded against the rock. These occur at various heights because the lake level rose and fell as the climate changed.

Dry River Canyon

Dry River Canyon is a deep, dramatic gorge cutting a zigzag course through Horse Ridge, a mountain east of Bend. It was the outlet for the prehistoric Lake Millican. Originally water from this basin flowed to the south of Horse Ridge, but as Newberry Volcano grew, lava flows dammed this drainage, forming Lake Millican. The climate at that time was wetter, so there was plenty of rainwater to fill the lake. Also, Newberry Volcano was covered with glaciers, and their melt water helped feed the lake. During high water periods, the lake drained through a

Dry River Canyon.

new route over Horse Ridge, eroding a canyon. The water then flowed north to the Crooked River, where it eventually entered the Columbia. At the lower mouth of the canyon is a large fan of sand and gravel which is mined today to maintain Highway 20.

The canyon makes for interesting hiking. Park at the bottom and, with a little exploring, you'll find a trail that follows the ancient river bed up the canyon. Up to 300 feet in depth, the canyon provides shelter for a juniper forest and even a few ponderosa pines. The canyon is closed to entry from February to August to protect nesting birds. (Contact the BLM for current closure information.)

Crack in the Ground

If you are hiking just north of the town Christmas Valley, you'd better watch where you step. Lurking in what appears to be a broad, flat plain is a narrow, deep chasm. You would never know it was there until you came upon its edge.

This odd formation is Crack in the Ground, a two-mile long fault in the earth's crust. As its name implies, this fissure is simply a large crack, called a tension fracture. This area is at the northern portion of a region in the Great Basin where rock is under stress. At key

Crack in the Ground.

points, the stress is so great that the ground literally tears open from the tension, creating a fault. (It's similar to cracks that form on the surface of banana bread as it rises during baking.) Normally these cracks fill with rubble; Crack in the Ground is unusual because it has remained open for 1,000 years.

Crack in the Ground is two miles long, up to 70 feet deep, and up to 15 feet wide. It's so deep in places that it traps cold air, keeping winter ice frozen well into the summer. Homesteaders used to harvest this ice. A maze of trails allows you to explore this formation from every angle.

Newberry Volcano

South of Bend is one of the largest volcanoes in the continental United States. It is so huge that from a distance, it looks more like a mountain range than a single volcano. It's up to 30 miles in diameter and 500 square miles in size.

Along with its size, Newberry is unique in that it exhibits almost every known volcanic feature. It's a hodgepodge of obsidian flows, lava tubes, cinder cones, ash deposits, lava domes, and much more. To use another ice cream analogy, it's like a giant ice cream sundae made with a scoop of every flavor. In fact, there's such variety that some geologists suggest Newberry is a volcanic field, consisting of several, independent volcanoes. A volcanologist would never get bored here!

Newberry is a shield volcano; instead of steep conical peak, the mountain has gently sloping sides. From a distance, this type of

The caldera of Newberry Volcano with Paulina Lake, East Lake, Paulina Peak, and Big Obsidian Flow.

volcano looks like a shield resting on the ground.

At the summit is a five-mile-wide caldera containing two lakes. It formed 80,000 years ago when a large eruption drained the enormous magma chamber below the mountain. The chamber collapsed, taking the mountain peak with it, forming a large caldera. This is the same process that formed Crater Lake, and there is evidence that a similar lake existed at Newberry. But over the centuries, smaller eruptions filled in the crater with lava, raising its floor high enough so that the two current lakes can now drain through a creek that flows over the lowest part of the caldera wall.

Newberry Volcano was designated a national monument in 1990 to preserve and protect the area's unique features. It is managed by the

Cinder cones dotting the flanks of Newberry.

US Forest Service. There's plenty to see when you visit. A viewpoint is located at Paulina Peak, the highest point on the crater wall at 7,985 feet. The flanks of the volcano are peppered with 400 cinder cones, more than any other volcano in the world. Many lava tubes snake down the sides of the mountain, several of which you can visit. Inside the crater, along with the two lakes, are a cinder cone and a fascinating obsidian flow. A trail leads into the flow, which at first glance looks like a typical lava flow. However, this one contains chunks and ribbons of glassy obsidian twisted throughout the lava.

Obsidian.

Newberry Volcano is far from being dormant. It's a new volcano that formed less than a million years ago. The Big Obsidian Flow was the most recent eruption, which occurred 1,300 years ago (not very long in geologic time). Magma is close to the surface and is a potential source of geothermal power. A test well drilled in 1981 found 510° F water 3,057 feet under the surface. That is hotter than the water found at The Geysers in California, currently the world's largest geothermal-powered, electrical generating complex. Efforts are currently underway at Newberry to tap into this potential powerhouse of pollution free energy.

Lava Cast Forest

About seven thousand years ago, an eruption released a lava flow off the western flank of Newberry Volcano. This fluid lava poured downhill into a forest. As the lava surrounded living trees, moisture in the trunks cooled the lava quickly, creating crusts, or molds, of

Lava cast.

the tree trunks. The trees themselves burned away, leaving trunk-shaped holes in the lava flow.

Today, you can explore this ancient forest. If you look closely at the inside of the molds, you may see details of the tree trunks frozen into the lava. Several types of formations are visible:

Lava "trees" – Lava surrounded the trunk, hardening into a mold. If the lava flow then dropped the mold was left as a hollow tube sticking up into the air.

Horizontal molds – The trees sometimes fell, either because fast-moving lava toppled the tree or the base of the trunk burned through. As with the vertical trees, the lava cooled and the tree burned away; but this time a horizontal mold was created.

With all this talk about tree molds, why is this site called Lava Cast Forest? A cast is produced when a mold is filled with material, then the mold is removed. That's how plaster statues are made. If you cover an object with material, then remove the object, the material forms a mold which retains the outer shape of the object. So, technically, this place should be called the Lava Mold Forest!

Lava Tubes

Even though lava tubes are common throughout Central Oregon, they are still exotic and mysterious. There's something adventurous about climbing down into the bowels of the earth into a pitch black, eerily silent realm. But turn on your flashlight and a wonderful subterranean world opens up before you.

As the name implies, a lava tube is simply a tube-shaped cave inside a lava flow. It's more austere than a limestone cavern, without exotic formations or a maze of interconnected rooms. Some lava tubes have branching corridors, but that's unusual. However, a lava tube's simplicity is what makes it so accessible. You don't need special climbing equipment, you can't get lost underground, and hiking a lava tube is relatively safe.

Lava tubes are created during volcanic eruptions. During an eruption, fluid lava flows downhill in channels or "rivers". Exposed to cool air, the lava on the surface solidifies, forming an insulating "roof." Below this roof, the lava river continues to flow freely. The eruption continues in cycles and the lava level rises and falls in the tube depending on volcanic output. But the tube itself remains intact due to the insulating layers of solidified lava surrounding it. Eventually, the eruption stops, and the lava drains out the lower end of the tube, leaving a hollow, underground chamber.

Exploring the subterranean world of a lava tube.

Lava tubes are not outrageously decorated with formations like a limestone cavern. But as you explore a lava tube, you will see formations that allow you to "read" the story of what happened inside. Here are a few to look for:

Flow marks – If you visit a reservoir in late summer, you'll see bands along the shoreline marking the water level as it slowly receded over the season. Lava tubes have similar bands, called flow marks, that show the different lava levels in the tube.

Benches – Sometimes you'll see a long "bench" on either side of the lava tube, a few feet above the floor. These formed as the lava flow reduced to a thin stream. Wherever the lava touched the cooler rock, it solidified, forming benches and creating an ever narrowing channel. Stand on a bench and imagine a glowing, red river of lava flowing by. (In the lava tube photo, note the bench on the left side.)

Lava tube liner – As the eruption progressed, waves of lava would flow through the tube. Since the walls are cooler than the flow, some lava would solidify in a thin film on the wall, leaving layers. Subsequent flows built up the layers like an onion. After the tube drained and the lava cooled, some of these layers broke off as large, flat plates. You will see these plates on the floor and a matching flat hole in the wall.

Lavacicles – As the eruption waned, the lava level dropped inside the tube, leaving a gap between the flow and the ceiling. The intense heat from the lava flow re-melted the roof, causing roof material to sag and drip. The end result is a smooth, glassy surface with "drips" of lava hanging down.

Roof collapse – Don't worry, these didn't happen recently! After the lava drained out, the walls cooled and contracted. During this cooling, stresses in the rock created cracks and sections collapsed into large boulder piles on the floor. In fact, you probably entered the tube in a section where the roof was so thin, the collapse created an opening to the surface.

The temperature in a lava tube remains constant year round because

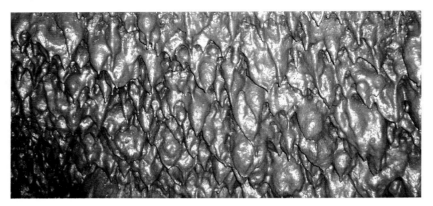

Lavacicle formations in a lava tube.

of the insulating rock around the cave. Over time, the temperature in a cave equalizes to the average temperature of the climate. In Central Oregon, cave temperatures hover around 40-45 degrees Fahrenheit. As a result, our caves feel cool in the summer and warm in the winter.

Lava tubes can be found throughout Central Oregon. Many are on the slopes of Newberry Volcano, but they can also be found in Bend, near Sisters, near the Redmond Airport, and other areas. There are even two houses in Bend built above a lava tube! One has a fan that uses air from the cave to cool the house in the summer. How's that for a huge basement?

The easiest cave to explore is Lava River Cave near Sunriver. It's run by the Forest Service and admission is free (there is a parking fee). This is the largest, most spectacular lava tube in Central Oregon and it contains plenty of interesting formations. Lanterns are available for rent at the site, but I feel they ruin the experience when you are exploring inside. With a good flashlight (one per person, plus extras as backup) you can actually see more, since your night vision isn't disrupted by a bright lantern. You can also contact local tour companies to explore other caves. But if you do explore a cave on your own, please don't smoke, litter, light fires, damage formations, bring a dog, smash bottles, collect rocks, etc. The Forest Service is starting to close down caves because of damage caused by visitors – an unfortunate necessity.

Cinder Cones

Central Oregon has an unusually dense concentration of cinder cones. The landscape is littered with 600 of these small volcanoes, many of which are located on the flanks of Newberry Volcano. Some are only a few dozen feet high, most are 300-500 feet high, and the highest is 800 feet.

A cinder cone is a small volcano that sprays blobs of lava from eruptions driven by pressurized gas. As the composition of Newberry's flanks suggests, cinder cones usually form as a side vent of the main volcano, creating a "volcano on a volcano."

During the eruption, lava blobs fly through the air and cool. As they cool, dissolved gasses bubble out, creating light, frothy cinders. The cinders pile up and stick together, forming a steep sided cone, usually with a crater at the top. Depending on the prevailing wind, the cones may be symmetrical or elongated on the downwind side. An eruption lasts from a few weeks to a few years, and near the end, a lava flow often bursts out of the lower side of the cinder cone because there isn't enough gas pressure to blow cinders into the air.

Among the hundreds of cinder cones in the Central Oregon, two are readily accessible to the public. Lava Butte is located just off of Highway 97 south of Bend. This 500-foot-high cone erupted seven

Lava Butte. Note the lava flow off the left side.

thousand years ago. There's a parking area, visitor center, and a great interpretive trail allowing you explore the lava flow that originally gushed out the base. This flow created an enormous lava field which spread west, diverting the flow of the Deschutes River, and created Benham and Dillon Falls. A road leads to the top of the cone, which features a nice crater and fire lookout tower.

Another accessible cinder cone is 490-foot Pilot Butte, a popular landmark in Bend. A road and hiking trail lead to a summit viewpoint which offers the *best* panoramic views of Central Oregon.

Pilot Butte in Bend.

Volcano Guide

Most people think of a volcano as a steep sided cone with lava gushing out the top. But volcanoes come in many shapes and forms. Here are a few major types found in Central Oregon:

Stratovolcano (or composite volcano) — This is the classic, cone-shaped, steep-sided volcano and is also the most common type. As its name implies, it's made up of layers (strata) of chunky rocks, grainy ash, and fluid lava. Good examples are the peaks of the High Cascades, such as the Sisters and Mt. Jefferson.

Shield volcano — This is the classic Hawaiian volcano and it looks like a shield lying on the ground. These volcanoes erupt a fluid lava that flows away quickly, creating a gently sloped mountain. Belknap Crater and Awbrey Butte in Bend are good examples.

Cinder cone — A small volcano, usually about 300-500 feet high. Lava under pressure sprays into the air, cools, and then falls as frothy cinders. Eventually, the cinders pile up to form a steep sided cone, with a crater on top. There are hundreds of cinder cones in the area, but Lava Butte and Pilot Butte are the most visited.

Flood basalt — An unusual volcano that doesn't form a mountain. It's simply a crack in the ground that disgorges enormous amounts of lava. The lava is so fluid that, instead of forming a mountain, it flows away as a flood inundating the landscape. One of the world's largest basalt floods occurred in Eastern Oregon and Washington. While the fissures that released the lava are no longer visible, you can still see the hardened lava of the floods themselves. These can be seen in the steep cliff walls along the Columbia River.

Lava dome — Lava Domes are formed from sticky, thick lava. Oozing out a volcanic vent like toothpaste, the lava forms dome-shaped blobs. The Big Obsidian flow and Paulina Peak at Newberry Caldera are lava domes. Just off the northwest end of Sparks Lake is an interesting string of lava domes called "Devil's Garden" on the slopes of South Sister.

Caldera — A caldera is the result of a catastrophic eruption of a shield or stratovolcano. The eruption is so forceful that it drains the magma chamber located under the mountain. Once empty, the peak of the mountain (or the part that hasn't already blown off) collapses into this giant chamber, creating a vast crater called a caldera. Crater Lake and Newberry Volcano both have classic calderas.

Supervolcano — These are volcanoes on a massive scale, both in size and power. Their eruptions are so powerful that they devastate the landscape for hundreds of miles and can change the climate globally. The town of Prineville sits in the Crooked River Caldera and Smith Rock is a formation along its rim. This caldera is twenty miles in diameter, and is four times larger than Newberry's caldera.

Plants

Plants take center stage in Central Oregon. Our towns were founded on agriculture, ranching, and logging. Today, a major portion of the local economy is driven by tourism, vacation homes, and retirement living. People are drawn to this region by the dramatic and varied scenery. There are several types of forests, lush river ecosystems, and broad brushy plains. You can never get bored and it's all stunningly beautiful.

Our plants do more than passively provide a pretty backdrop. They aggressively fight for survival in this arid climate. Junipers suck up available water, keeping competing plants at bay. Conifers fight off bark beetles by flooding boreholes with sap. Manzanita thrive on forest fires. At the same time, plants provide food and homes for animals and some even fertilize the ground. The plants in Central Oregon are aggressive and dynamic, always active in their struggle for survival.

Opposite page: Juniper near Gray Butte.

The Role of Plants

Plants play an active role in the environment and humans wouldn't be around without them. Consider these facts:

- Plants (and fungi) were the first organisms to colonize land. Only then could animals follow.

- Plants form the base of the food chain because they can make their own food using sunlight. Animals can't produce their own food so must eat. They consume either plants or animals that eat plants.

- Oxygen comes from plants. Surprisingly, most of our oxygen does not come from rain forests but from microscopic, single celled algae living in the oceans. Yes, they're small; but remember that oceans cover three quarters of the planet. Certain microorganisms also produce oxygen.

- Plants affect the climate. They absorb greenhouse gasses, they affect the amount of sunlight reflected from the earth's surface, and they influence humidity in entire regions. For example, in the Amazon, downpours are partly fed by moisture released from the jungle.

- Plants engage in biochemical warfare. Since they can't run away from herbivores, plants produce toxins, resins, and other chemicals to keep from being eaten. Our sagebrush contains noxious oil that tastes horrible. Many medicines come from these powerful chemicals produced by plants.

- Plants can define an entire economy. Bend relied on the timber industry for decades. Now its economy is supported by tourism, as people are increasingly attracted to the beautiful forests and scenery.

- Plants provide shelter and homes for animals. For example, quail nest in bitterbrush. Humans are no exception – isn't your house made mostly from wood?

What is a Plant?

What exactly is a plant? It's not as easy to define as you'd think. For example, you may say that plants are green. Well, that would exclude red plum trees and imply that green parrots are plants. You could say that a plant grows in the ground. Does that make clams plants and floating algae animals? Hmmm...defining a plant is not as easy as it seems.

Is this organism a plant just because it's green?

Botanists have identified characteristics that define plants. The first two are unique to the Plant Kingdom:

- **Cell walls** – Plant cells are surrounded by stiff, cellulose walls. That's why they don't need skeletons.

- **Unlimited growth** – Most animals grow to a specific size then stop. (Have you ever seen a five pound mouse?) Plants grow continuously until their death, which is why you can find ponderosa trees two inches or two hundred feet tall in the same forest.

Plants have other characteristics, but some of these aren't exclusive to the plant kingdom:

- **Photosynthesis** – Plants use chlorophyll to produce sugar from sunlight, carbon dioxide, and water. Since they manufacture their own food, plants don't need to eat. However, plants without chlorophyll exist; these are parasites which steal sugars produced by other plants. There are also organisms, such as protozoa and bacteria, that contain chlorophyll and produce sugars just like plants. So if it's green and needs sunlight, it's not necessarily a plant!

- **Immobile** - Plants do not have muscles, can't move, and are (usually) rooted to one spot. Despite this, plants do move a little bit. They can gradually lean or move their leaves towards the sun. And yes, there is such a thing as a "walking" tree! In Costa Rica there's a tree that moves through the forest by growing roots to one side of its trunk while letting the roots on the other side die off. It's not very fast, but in a few months, the tree can move a few inches.

- **Lack of nervous system or muscles** – Since plants are usually rooted to one spot, they don't need systems for locomotion. Yet plants aren't completely "unaware" of their environments. They respond to light, drought, heat, cold, insect attacks, and other factors. For example, plants "know" when to drop their leaves in the fall and when to bloom in the spring.

The Food Chain

Plants form the foundation of the food chain by taking energy from sunlight and storing it in sugars. Herbivores eat plants and use those sugars to "power" their bodies. Carnivores then eat the herbivores. Energy from sunlight moves up the food chain, "powering" all the animals in turn. You could say that all these organisms are solar

powered! If plants disappeared, most life on earth would vanish. If animals disappeared, plants would do just fine!

Did you know plants are made from air and water? Most people assume that the structure of a plant is extracted from nutrients in the soil. Yet interestingly, almost the entire plant is made from carbon dioxide and water. Only trace

The leaves of plants act as solar collectors.

Ft. Rock looms above a plain of rabbitbrush. Despite the region's aridity, plants thrive.

amounts of nutrients are taken from the soil. If a ponderosa seedling is planted in a pot filled with a ton of soil, several years later the resulting tree will weigh hundreds of pounds but the pot will still contain almost a ton of soil.

Surviving in an Arid Climate

Plants in our region employ various strategies to survive scant rainfall, harsh sun, bitter cold, and dry air. As you explore the plants in Central Oregon, look for the characteristics described below. Some plants may use several of these strategies:

Store water - Plants can store water from infrequent rains in specialized roots, stems, and leaves. For example, Central Oregon succulents store water in fat, juicy leaves and stems.

Grow small or no leaves - Water exits a plant through its leaves; plants with smaller leaves or none at all reduce their water loss. Juniper leaves are so small they've been reduced to scales.

Protect the leaves - Some plants, such as manzanita, have leaves with a thick, waxy coating to prevent water loss. Other plants, such as mullein, are covered with fine hairs which perform several functions. They shade the plant from sunlight. They also create an insulating dead air space close to the plants, protecting them from intense heat and reducing evaporation. In addition, hairs (and thorns)

The leaves of sagebrush are covered in tiny hairs that reflect sun. Oils in the leaves taste awful, discouraging herbivores.

discourage herbivores (who wants a mouthful of hair?)

Avoid dry spells - Some plants go dormant in dry conditions to take advantage of infrequent rains. Plants take advantage of dormancy in various ways:

- Drop leaves and re-grow them when rains come.

- Grow, flower, and produce seeds quickly before conditions become dry. The seeds lie dormant, possibly for several years, until the right amount of rain comes. Many of our annual flowers grow in spring when it's wet and finish flowering before the surrounding environment dries out in July.

Fancy roots - Some plants grow roots outward in a shallow, fibrous mat in order to catch every drop of what little rain falls. Others grow deep, long tap roots in search of a permanent source of groundwater. Sagebrush, which grows both types of roots, are very successful in arid climates.

Taste bad - In a desert full of hungry and thirsty herbivores, a plant survives more easily if it tastes bad. Many desert plants are loaded with bitter-tasting aromatic oils for this reason. Sagebrush uses this strategy; its pungent aroma comes from these aromatic oils.

Disturbance Forests

In arid climates, plants are threatened by wildfires. To cope, the forests of Central Oregon have adapted to thrive on fires. Our forests are considered "disturbance forests", a term describing a forest ecosystem in constant flux and one which requires occasional disease or fire to remain healthy.

Most people think of a healthy forest as an established old growth forest, with giant towering trees. But death, disease, and fires are all part of a normal ecosystem and organisms have adapted to and even require these events for survival. If humans could somehow protect forests so every tree becomes mature, havoc would be wreaked on the ecosystem. Let's see why.

In a typical cycle, as trees reach maturity, they become weaker and unable to fight off beetle infestations. The beetles thrive (along with the woodpeckers that eat them) but the forest slowly dies off. The dead snags provide shelter for animals and decaying trees provide nutrients and organic matter which build up soils. The dead forest is susceptible to fires, which many of our plants need to reproduce. Heat cracks open hard seed coats, allowing plants to germinate, and the ash fertilizes the soil. After a fire, sunny open meadows appear providing a wealth of food for wildlife, room for young trees to flourish, and serving as a firebreak that protects adjacent forests from advancing wildfires. Eventually, a young forest starts actively growing, absorbing tons of carbon dioxide and providing multiple habitats and food sources for animals. As this forest matures, habitats and animal populations change accordingly. A healthy ecosystem would appear as a patchwork of meadows, young and old forest and dead snags.

In the western United States, a lot of politics surrounds logging and wildfire suppression. But I believe the dynamic nature of our forests can provide win-win solutions for both environmentalists and industry. For example, prudent logging can reduce fuel loads for wildfire and stimulate the growth of new, young forests. Meanwhile, other stands of valuable timber can be left untouched to mature into old growth forests. The U.S. Forest Service was founded to manage our forests sustainably, balancing the needs of the environment and industry. Some critics question their decisions, but the Forest Service employees I've met are intelligent, educated, and very aware of the issues. I find that reassuring and I'm optimistic about the future of our forests.

Plant Regions

As you travel through Central Oregon, you'll notice that the scenery changes often. One minute you are driving through forest; then suddenly the landscape opens to a shrubby plain. This variety is what makes the area so interesting. If you get bored with arid flatlands, cool alpine forest is less than an hour's drive away.

This variety is created by a combination of factors such as altitude, water, temperature, microclimate, soils, rainfall, and sunlight. For example, Bend and Redmond are both arid because the Cascades block Pacific storms. But Bend is at a higher elevation, so receives a few more inches of rainfall, enough to support ponderosa forests. The result is a region made up of a patchwork of ecosystems, mainly defined by plant type. Here are a few examples:

Riparian — This is just a fancy term for an ecosystem next to water. Plant communities are made up of willow, alder, red-osier dogwood, and sedges. You can see these plants along the Deschutes River Trail, Shevlin Park, and the river canyons north of Bend. In the drier river canyons, the riparian zone is like an oasis where dusky desert scrub gives way to a lush green community of trees.

Great basin — The southernmost parts of this region butt against the edge of the Great Basin Desert and have a similar ecosystem. It's dry, open land with no trees, but covered with sagebrush, rabbitbrush, and bunch grasses. Fort Rock Valley and the areas around Millican are good examples of this type of ecosystem.

Juniper woodlands — The plains north and east of Bend are covered with the largest juniper woodland in North America. It consists of juniper trees with an understory of sagebrush and bunch grass.

Ponderosa forest — The areas to the south and west of Bend are covered with ponderosa pine forest. It's a beautiful, open forest, carpeted with manzanita, bitterbrush, bunch grass, and snowbrush.

Lodgepole forest — The area around LaPine is a flat plain with a cool, high-elevation climate, perfect for lodgepole pines. Sunriver is also located in a lodgepole forest.

High elevation — At high elevations, above five thousand feet or so, are forests of firs, hemlock, and white bark pine. These forests can be found in the Cascades and near the summit of Newberry Volcano.

Some Plants of Central Oregon

This section highlights a few common plants found in Central Oregon and provides instructions for finding them. Identification should be easy; most are so common you'll practically trip over them when you get out of your car.

Ponderosa Pine

Ponderosa is a majestic tree that grows throughout the western United States, and is very common in this area. In a mature ponderosa forest, two things are striking: the orange bark and the open, park-like meadows beneath the trees. The first is a mystery; foresters don't know what causes the bark of a mature ponderosa to turn from gray to orange. No other conifer has orange bark. But the second is very important; ponderosas have evolved to live with fire. The trees grow tall, have thick bark, and are self-pruning (the lower branches naturally fall off). As a result, when fire spreads across the forest floor, flames are unable to reach the crown and kill the tree. The fires clear out underbrush, leaving an open, park-like forest. Seeds sprout in the fertile soil

and the young trees now have the light and space they need to become established. The forest floor eventually becomes repopulated with bitterbrush, manzanita, snowbrush, and bunch grasses.

Ponderosas are the second most important timber tree in the United States (after Douglas fir) and supported the lumber mills in Bend for many years. They can live for 400-500 years and have deep roots to keep them from falling over. If you see a mature tree, take a close look at the cracked, orange, jigsaw-puzzle bark. If you place

your nose in a deep crack and take a sniff, you'll smell vanilla or butterscotch. That's because conifers contain chemicals used to make imitation vanilla, which is produced as a byproduct of the paper industry.

Expansive ponderosa forests are found to the south and west of Bend. Great places to

Jigsaw puzzle bark.

experience these trees include the Deschutes River trail, along Century Drive (on the way to Mt. Bachelor), and in Shevlin Park. The most spectacular forests are northwest of Sisters near Black Butte. There you'll see the classic orange bark, massive towering trees, and an open forest floor. You can also find isolated stands of ponderosas in the deep river canyons to the north.

It's very easy to identify a mature ponderosa. The bark is orange, it flakes off in pieces that look like a jigsaw puzzle, and has deep, black grooves. No branches grow on the lower trunk, giving the tree a tall, clean look. A younger tree is harder to identify since the lower limbs haven't fallen off yet and the bark is a flaky gray-brown color. But if you see a pine tree in the locations mentioned above and it has long needles in clusters of three, it's a ponderosa.

Western Juniper

Another common tree is the juniper. It has a large root system that extends out beyond the crown to collect scant moisture. As a result, it out-competes other plants, gobbling up available water. The result is a unique-looking, open woodland. When visiting Bend, the

author David Sedaris commented on our interesting forests of short, widely spaced trees. The audience laughed, thinking Sedaris was joking; but he was honestly noting how strikingly beautiful and unusual a juniper woodland can be.

Juniper is a conifer (like a pine tree); but instead of needles, its leaves have been reduced to resinous scales that produce a strong, pleasant scent. The small scales are an adaptation to prevent water loss. Juniper is not a good tree for commercial harvest. The branches are twisted, rough, branch often and taper quickly; the bark makes deep inclusions into the wood, and when dried, the wood buckles. These are not qualities lumbermen desire. Most of the junipers in Central Oregon are less than one hundred years old, but a 1,600 year old tree has been found on Horse Ridge, east of Bend. Junipers produce blue-gray berries in late summer. These "berries" are in fact cones (junipers are conifers, and as the name implies, they produce cones). Birds and other animals eat the berries, which dissolve in their stomachs releasing the seeds, which in turn are deposited in their poop, helping the forest to spread. There is an interesting commercial use for juniper berries; they are used to flavor gin.

An extensive juniper forest can be found to the east of Bend, spreading up to Redmond. It's considered to be the largest juniper woodland in the United States. The trees are widely spaced amid a carpet of sagebrush and bunch grasses. They are incredibly easy to identify; any tree between Bend and Redmond is most likely a juniper. The trees have a gnarly, twisted trunk and green scales instead of needles. They also emit a wonderful, resinous smell.

Despite their beauty, these dense forests may not be natural. Historic photos of the region show widely scattered, individual trees, not the woodlands that exist today. Scientists suspect that this is due to favorable weather conditions and extensive fire suppression over the last 150 years. While the result is wonderful woodlands, the density encourages mistletoe infestations that kill trees.

Fir trees

A fir tree is a conifer, like a pine; but instead of long needles, firs have short, stubby ones. Firs are commonly used as Christmas trees.

They grow at higher elevations, and can be found in areas of Central Oregon that are between four and six thousand feet in elevation. In an established forest, seedlings have a hard time getting enough light to grow. But once established, firs are shade-tolerant and are common in mature forests. The wood of fir is soft and not very

strong, so it's mainly used for making paper or constructing pack-ing crates. They are also used as Christmas trees and for ornamental landscaping.

Our two major types of fir are white fir and grand fir. But in the mountains west of Central Oregon, something unusual has hap-pened to these trees. The two species have hybridized into a tree that shows characteristics of both. It's possible for two foresters to examine the same tree and for one to conclude that it's a white fir while the other declares it a grand fir. These trees are large, grow-ing 130-160 feet tall with trunks up to six feet in diameter. Their leaves are blue-green.

Firs can be found at the highest elevations of Newberry Volcano as well as the High Cascades, such as around Mt. Bachelor. To iden-tify them, look for a tree that has leaves resembling a Christmas tree. The needles will be short and stubby, not long and slender like a pine. Also, fir needles always occur individually, not in bundles as pine needles do. Fir resin gives the forest a wonderfully refresh-ing, alpine smell.

Lodgepole Pine

The Lodgepole Pine is a tall, slender tree, often seventy-five feet tall but only a foot in diameter. Indians used the thin trunks as poles to hold up their conical tents (thus the term "lodgepole.")

Lodgepoles are like the rabbits of the conifer world because they reproduce so prolifically. Seedlings grow rapidly, trees start producing cones earlier than other conifers, and they spread huge quantities of seed. Lodgepoles crowd out other conifers and dominate the forest. Mountain pine beetles attack these dense stands with vigor, killing trees, and making the forest susceptible to wildfire. Unlike the bark of a ponderosa, a lodgepole's bark is thin and not fire-resistant; so a fire usually destroys the trees. Surprisingly, that's an advantage. The fire melts resin that glues the cones shut, releasing seeds. The seedlings have a clear, sunny space to grow, and rapidly build up a new forest.

Lodgepole wood is versatile, and is used to make railroad ties, mine timbers, lumber, firewood, knotty pine paneling, fence posts, corral rails, and, not surprisingly, telephone poles.

Lodgepoles are found in Sunriver and LaPine. The best way to identify them is to look for needles growing in pairs. They are shorter than ponderosa needles and sharper. The trees are tall and slender with gray, scaly bark.

Willow

A common willow in this area is the yellow willow. It is a tree, but looks like a big shrub with many branches. The leaves, which fall

Willow trees look like shrubs along the river.

off in winter, are a yellow-green color. It grows rapidly up to a height of sixteen feet. Yellow willows often dominate flat areas near rivers and streams where the ground is moist and silty. Their roots stabilize stream banks, helping to prevent erosion. The trees help aquatic animals by providing food and places to hide; they also shade the water, cooling it off on hot summer days.

Native Americans found many uses for the yellow willow. Its branches and bark can be used to weave baskets and make ropes. The bark also contains salicylic acid, the main ingredient in aspirin. People used to chew on the bark to relieve aches and pains.

Willows can be found near rivers at the bottoms of arid canyons in the northern part of Central Oregon. It's notoriously hard to identify

individual willow species, but if you see a willow in this region, it's most likely a yellow willow. The tree itself is shrubby, made up of many branches. The yellow-green leaves are elongated with a different shade of color on one side, and a sharp tip. They are found in flat areas along water, where the soil is silty.

Alder

Our predominant alder is the mountain alder (also known as the thin leaf alder). Like the willow, this shrubby tree lives near streams and loses its leaves in the winter. Unlike the willow, it grows farther away from the stream in gravelly soils and on steeper slopes. It can grow up to thirty feet tall.

The roots of alder contain lumps full of nitrogen-fixing bacteria. These nodules are fertilizer factories, in which bacteria convert nitrogen from the air into a form that can be used by plants. Other plants grow near alders to take advantage of this nutrient source. Native Americans pounded alder wood to make a red dye.

Just like willows, alders can be found near any river, and can be seen at the Deschutes River trail, Shevlin Park, or along canyon bottoms. Look for a shrubby tree up to thirty feet high, with smooth, gray bark. The trees like wet soil near streams and prefer gravelly soils with little silt. The leaves, which can grow up to four inches long, are an oval heart shape, have toothed edges, and a pale underside.

Red-osier Dogwood

Those familiar with dogwood trees and their beautiful white blooms may be disappointed in this plant. Its flowers are smaller and not as

showy as a traditional dogwood. But the red-osier dogwood makes up for that with striking, bright red stems which provide intense color during the winter when its leaves fall off. These colorful stems, combined with beautiful green foliage during the summer, make this a popular plant for landscaping in the region.

Red-osier dogwood lives in swampy thickets or near stream sides. It's a small shrub that can grow six to sixteen feet in height. You can easily identify this plant in the winter, as the red stems stand out among the gray twigs of other plants. But in summer, all the other plants leaf out, and the red-osier dogwood can get lost in the dense thicket. You may have to poke about in the foliage to find the red stems.

It produces long, straight, slender shoots, which made it ideal for Native Americans to use as skewers, roasting racks, and drying stretchers for salmon. They also smoked the bark.

You can find red-osier dogwood near any stream or river in Central Oregon. Good places to look include along the Deschutes River trail, in Shevlin Park near Tumalo creek, and in the river canyons north of Bend.

Bitterbrush

A rose bush in the desert? Bitterbrush is a member of the plant family that includes roses, but it's more of a distant cousin than an actual rose. Our bitterbrush grows as shrubs three to five feet high and is most often found in the open understory of ponderosa pine forests. During winter, the leaves fall off and the bush is an ugly, dry,

twiggy mass. But in summer, it is covered with tiny, dark green leaves shaped like little duck feet, and blooms with pale yellow or pink flowers in late spring. The slight fuzz on the leaves reflects sunlight, keeping the plant cool and preventing water loss. Its name comes from its bitter-tasting leaves.

Bitterbrush is highly flammable and is destroyed by fire. So why does it live in ponderosa forests, which are adapted to frequent fires? It turns out that bitterbrush is also fire-dependant. The fires clear out forest floor litter, allowing new seedlings to sprout. Oddly enough, the seeds sprout from underground caches collected by rodents. So a fire now and then actually helps bitterbrush populations.

Bitterbrush serves many roles in the ecosystem. It is an important food source for deer, elk, antelope, and even livestock. It's so popular as food that these animals keep wild bitterbrush neatly pruned as they nibble away. This plant grows well in dry, rocky soil, and its roots help bind the soil together, preventing erosion. Its roots host bacteria that convert nitrogen from the air into a fertilizer that can be used by plants. Finally, the dense shrubby nature of the plant provides protection for small animals.

Bitterbrush is very common, and can easily be found in the ponderosa forests south and west of Bend.

Snowbrush

Snowbrush is a low evergreen shrub that can grow up to six feet tall. The plant is formed from many stems that grow from its base. Shrubs often form large, dense colonies that grow up to thirty feet wide. The plant produces a strong odor like a sweet cigar; this is the origin of the plant's other name, tobacco brush.

Like most plants that grow in ponderosa forests, snowbrush is adapted to fire and thrives on it. Like bitterbrush, the plant itself is flammable and burns up in a fire. But it produces a seed with an extremely hard coat that can remain in the soil for years. For the plant to germinate, the seed coat needs to be cracked open, usually from the heat of fire. The fire burns off groundcover, providing an open area and plenty of sun for the seed to germinate. If the fire isn't too intense, a new plant can sprout from its existing root system. As the plant grows, it forms dense thickets, often keeping trees from becoming established. The result is an open, sunny area.

Snowbrush has a large taproot and a deep, spreading root system that reaches six to eight feet into the ground. These roots help prevent soil erosion, essential after a fire when there's no groundcover to protect the soil. The roots contain nodules of bacteria that convert nitrogen from air into fertilizer. This comes in handy after a fire, when soil nutrients have become depleted. The nitrogen fertilizer also helps other plants get reestablished. Snowbrush is a food source for deer, elk, quails, mourning doves, and small mammals.

To identify snowbrush, look for thickets of shrubs in open areas of the forest. The leaves are dark green, very shiny, oval, and tend to curl. Snowbrush has small white flowers grouped into fluffy tufts. These plants can be found in the forests west of Bend, along Century and Skyliner drives and along the Deschutes River Trail.

Sagebrush

Sagebrush is a common plant in the Columbia and Great Basins. It's so prolific, that settlers often described these areas as "an ocean of sagebrush" with plants carpeting the desert to the horizon. Despite its name, this is not the sage used in cooking, which is a member of the mint family. But sagebrush is related to seasoning; it's in the same family as tarragon.

Sagebrush grows as an evergreen bush that can reach four feet in height. But in ideal conditions, it can grow into a small tree of up to fifteen feet. The silvery leaves are covered with fine hairs, shading them from hot sun and preventing water loss.

The most distinctive feature of the plant is its wonderful, resin-like smell, especially strong after a rain or if its leaves are crushed. The odor comes from toxic, aromatic volatile oils found in the leaves. The smell and bitter taste discourage herbivores. Sagebrush is par-

ticularly harmful to cattle. If a cow eats too much of it, the oils kill off digestive organisms in its gut and the animal could starve, despite a belly-full of nutritious forage. While other animals can eat sagebrush, they prefer not to. The exceptions are pronghorn antelope and sage grouse, which seem to be immune to the oils and love eating the plant. The sage grouse not only uses it for up to seventy-five percent of its diet, but also nests in the plant.

Sagebrush is slightly toxic to humans. It may cause a skin reaction in sensitive individuals and it's definitely not something to eat. Native Americans used this plant as medicine, to make a yellow-gold dye, and for ritual purposes.

Sagebrush can be found practically everywhere in Central Oregon, with the exception of high elevation forests. It's especially prevalent in the grasslands and juniper woodlands north and east of Bend, but can also be found in forests. Look for a plant with silver-gray leaves that give off a pleasant odor when crushed. My favorite place to see sagebrush is the rest stop off of Highway 97, at the Crooked River Bridge viewpoint. For some reason, they seem to smell better there.

Manzanita

Manzanita is one of our most beautiful shrubs. It's an evergreen bush that grows to about three feet tall. It has woody, orange-red twisting branches with stiff, disk-shaped, waxy leaves. From May to July, it produces clusters of small, white, urn-shaped flowers.

Later in the season, the flowers produce the small, edible fruits which gave the plant its name: "manzanita" is Spanish for "little apple."

Like most plants living in a ponderosa forest, manzanita is adapted to fire. Like snowbrush, the seeds are encased in an extremely durable coating. In order to germinate, the coat must be cracked open by the heat of fire. Manzanita also spreads when animals eat the fruit and their digestive enzymes weaken the seed coat. When the animals poop the seeds out, the plant can germinate, and gets a little fertilizer in the process.

The woody branches of manzanita are hard, durable, and smooth, leading to an interesting commercial use as parrot perches for the pet trade.

Manzanita is common throughout the west, but one species, the raven's manzanita, is among the rarest plants in the world. In 1987, only one plant of this species was known to exist, in a secret location of the Presidio in San Francisco.

Manzanita can be found carpeting the understory of ponderosa pine forests. It's especially prevalent in the forests west of Bend. Look for a shrub with woody, red branches and oval, waxy leaves.

Rabbitbrush

Rabbitbrush is similar to sagebrush and almost as common. Normally, it's an unremarkable, cold-tolerant shrub that grows to about three feet tall and drops its leaves in winter. But you'll definitely notice it during August and September when the plant puts out an explosion of bright yellow flowers. In some areas, the entire desert floor turns a brilliant yellow.

Rabbitbrush was useful to Native Americans as food and medicine. They made a golden dye from the flowers and, by adding minerals, they could make rust or green dyes. Their most interesting use of the plant was as a chewing gum. The plant produces a latex rubber which gives it its gum-like character. During World War II, latex rubber was in short supply, so scientists studied rabbitbrush as a possible replacement source.

As its name implies, rabbitbrush is the favorite food of jackrabbits. The flowers are also food source for pollinating insects and butterflies.

Rabbitbrush can be found wherever you find sagebrush. The best place to see this shrub is near Fort Rock in late August or early September when the valley floor is carpeted with brilliant, yellow blooms. Rabbitbrush has soft, extremely narrow leaves. one to three inches long. In contrast, sagebrush is a woodier plant with short, duck-foot shaped leaves.

Bunch Grass

There are two types of grasses in the world. One group forms a carpet-like sod which is perfect for lawns and golf courses. The other group, bunch grass, grows in individual clumps or tufts. The ge-

neric term "bunch grass" doesn't describe a specific plant; it's simply the name of a group of grasses that share this common characteristic.

Bunch grasses have roots that can grow six feet into the soil, allowing them to find water. Sod grasses have shallow roots and would die in our arid climate.

Bunch grass leaves die off every winter, leaving brown tufts; but in the spring, new leaves sprout. As the plant grows older, the size of its bunch increases to over one foot in diameter. The plants provide food, shelter, and hiding places for small animals. They also make great forage for deer, antelope, and livestock. Unfortunately, in areas overgrazed by livestock, bunch grass is being replaced by invasive cheatgrass.

Bunch grasses are found everywhere in Central Oregon, from ponderosa forests, juniper woodlands, open plains, to canyon bottoms. Just look for clumps of grass.

Mistletoe

We have lots of mistletoe in Central Oregon, and almost every type

of tree hosts its own species. But you may not recognize it, because our mistletoe looks very different from the European and East Coast varieties used as Christmas decorations. Holiday mistletoe has green, oval leaves and white berries, whereas ours are simply a pom-pom of yellow-green stems.

Mistletoe is a hemi-parasite, with modified roots that grow into the branches of a host tree, sucking out nutrients and water. If enough mistletoe infests the tree, it can weaken and die. But the mistletoe isn't a complete mooch; the stems contain chlorophyll, so the plant can perform photosynthesis and produce sugars on its own.

To reproduce, mistletoe produces fruits which attract birds. The fruits contain seeds surrounded by sticky goo. The bird scatters the seed as it eats (birds are sloppy feeders) or it poops the seeds out. The sticky goo allows the seed to stick to a branch, and as the goo dries, it glues the seed to the branch.

Mistletoe can be seen as good or bad, depending on your point of view. It weakens trees and may kill them. But some studies show that juniper trees in woodlands infested with mistletoe produce more berries, attracting lots of birds. The birds eat the berries and spread the juniper seeds. Mistletoe also provides nesting material and high-quality food for animals. Mistletoe grows heavily in our juniper woodlands and its abundance is probably due to fire suppression. Without fires to thin the forests, trees grow closer together, facilitating the spread of mistletoe.

Juniper trees are the best places to look for mistletoe. The plants form yellow-green blobs in the trees. Awbrey Butte in Bend has many infested trees.

Plant Invaders

Several beautiful plant species living in Central Oregon are currently being destroyed through the activities of government, farmers, ranchers, and gardeners. Hopefully, if citizens speak up and take action, we can encourage this destruction and eliminate the plants completely. No, I'm not crazy. These particular plants are invasive weeds, plants from other regions that are taking over our ecosystem and displacing native plants. Many of these plants have beautiful leaves or bright, cheerful flowers, a fact which proves that beauty isn't always benign.

An invasive plant is a non-native that establishes itself aggressively in its new home, displacing native plants and harming agriculture and ranching. Such plants are imported accidentally (seeds contaminating a shipment of crop seed), or on purpose, (gardeners importing a pretty new flower). In their natural environments, these plants cause no problems because local pests and herbivores keep them under control. But these controlling factors are absent in a new environment, and the plants can take over.

Here are a few invasive plants found in the region. If you see one, go ahead and pull it up by its roots and throw it in the garbage.

Russian Thistle

Russian thistle is also known as tumbleweed, a plant that practically defines the American West. Few plants are as symbolically American. Unfortunately, tumbleweed is as American as the Eiffel Tower, tacos, or soy sauce. It's native to the Ural Mountains in Russia.

Tumbleweed was first introduced in South Dakota in 1877 as a stowaway in a shipment of flax seed from the Ukraine. The U.S. Department of Agriculture also planted tumbleweed as a source of forage for livestock. Since then, tumbleweed has thrived and spread across the entire western United States.

In the fall, the plant breaks off near the base, and the lightweight, twiggy, ball-shaped mass rolls away in the wind, dropping seeds along the way. A single plant can produce up to 200,000 seeds and since it's well adapted to arid environments, it thrives in the American West. No wonder it has become so common.

Tumbleweed causes many problems. It interferes with agriculture, depletes soil moisture, displaces native plants and shelters insect

pests and diseases. The dry balls collect on fences and create fire hazards. As the balls roll across highways, startled drivers may swerve dangerously to avoid hitting them. A funny sight common in the West is a car driving down the road with a big tumbleweed stuck under the front bumper.

You'll see tumbleweeds blowing around in areas north and east of Bend. They are often piled up along fences in agricultural areas.

Cheatgrass

This plant, native to the Mediterranean, has become one of the worst weedy grasses in the United States. As an agricultural weed, it can reduce crop yields of wheat, rye, and alfalfa by up to one third. In our ecosystem it out-competes and wipes out populations of bunch grass and native shrubs by using up all available soil moisture. It also out-competes by growing and flowering earlier in the season than native plants. The grass dries out quickly, providing fuel for wildfires. Cheatgrass provides poor forage for cattle, and when it grows in ranch areas the barbed seed heads can work their way into the nostrils, eyes, and hooves of livestock.

Cheatgrass is the one invasive plant that actually looks like a weed. It's a fuzzy grass that grows to about two feet tall. The stems end in thin leaves about six inches long. The flowers form many branching, soft, drooping tufts that turn a rusty red or purple. The seeds tend to stick in your socks and are hard to pull out. Cheatgrass is found everywhere in the region, but most often it grows where the soil has been disturbed, such as construction sites or agricultural areas.

Spotted Knapweed

This plant was probably introduced as a contaminant in crop seed imported from eastern Europe in the early 1900's. Spotted knapweed rapidly invades an area and chokes out native plants. It competes for water and nutrients and even produces a toxin to keep other plants from growing. The plant is a thistle and produces beautiful purple flowers of about a half-inch in diameter. The flowers bloom from buds covered with black spots. It has deeply lobed, pale green leaves that grow from one to three inches long. The bush grows from two to four feet tall and is comprised of thin, hairy, branched stems which give the plant an airy, open look. Spotted knapweed grows everywhere in the region, but is usually found along the sides of country roads and in empty city lots.

Dalmation Toadflax

This is a beautiful plant, related to a snapdragon, that produces cheerful, yellow flowers. Dalmation toadflax was imported as an ornamental plant from southeastern Europe in the mid 1800's. Once the plant is established, it can crowd out native species.

Toadflax grows as single or multiple stems up to three feet high.

The small leaves are light green, waxy, heart-shaped, and are attached directly to the main stem. The leaves alternate on the stem; each leaf grows a quarter of an inch above the previous one, but is displaced one third of the way around the stem. The leaves spiral up the entire stem in this pattern. The bright yellow flowers sprout from the leaf bases at the top third of the stems and look like snapdragons. Toadflax grows everywhere in the region (including my yard...sigh) and is most noticeable when it blooms in July.

Mullein

Mullein is a prolific seed-producer and will gradually take over an area if left uncontrolled. It also has a deep taproot, enabling it to out-compete other plants for water. Livestock won't eat mullein yet it displaces desirable forage plants. Mullein consists of a rosette of soft, wooly leaves near the ground and a two- to six-foot-tall stem, with a cluster of yellow flowers on top. There is some good news about this plant. It's not as aggressive as other invasive weeds and generally grows only in disturbed soils, such as roadsides, fields, and logged areas. It doesn't seem to venture out of those areas. Mullein is often found growing on the dirt shoulders of country roads. Just look for the tall stems and rosette of fuzzy leaves.

Animals

Central Oregon is full of wildlife. We have graceful antelope, adorable marmots, stinky skunks, fearsome rattlesnakes, cute quail, loud frogs, sleek fish, and annoying insects. Some of these creatures are easy to see; you might spot squirrels scampering through the forest or geese floating on a pond. But most animals prefer to stay hidden, and you'd be lucky to see one.

A Hidden Life

Most animals are secretive. Walking through a forest you may see a few dozen animals: mostly birds, perhaps a few squirrels, and if you are lucky, a deer or two. But during that stroll in the woods, you actually walked past thousands more animals. Didn't see them did you? What you missed are insects, worms, slugs, birds, frogs, snakes, salamanders, lizards, and big, furry animals that stayed well hidden.

Opposite page: Mule Deer.

Where are the animals? Thousands of animals are hidden in this typical forest scene.

Animals are shy to keep from being eaten. Most are food for other animals, and if you're lucky enough to be a predator, you still have to lay low because you need stealth to pursue your prey. Birds and insects aren't as shy as other animals, however, because they can fly from danger. Some strategies animals use for protection:

- **Movement** – Animals have the ability to move through their environment. So their number one strategy for survival is to move to a safe hiding place or run from danger. Plants can't move which is why they produce toxins and thorns.

- **Blending in** – Most animals are earth-toned to blend with their surroundings.

- **Nocturnal activity** – Many animals use the cover of darkness for protection. Likewise, predators are active at night because that's when their prey are exposed.

- **Hiding** – Many animals live under bark, under the forest duff, in burrows, under rocks, and inside dense bushes.

Considering the many ways animals conceal themselves, we are lucky to see them at all. The secret to spotting these animals is to look for them at dusk or dawn, when they are more active. (I occasionally see rabbits in my yard when I get the morning newspaper.)

Surviving a Dry Climate

Just as plants need adaptations for life in a dry climate, animals in Central Oregon need similar strategies. Even though they can move and search for water, that water may be scarce. Arid climates also experience extreme heat and cold, which present additional problems for animals. Here are some tricks they use to cope with the climate:

- **Avoiding the heat of day** - Many animals are nocturnal, active only at night. Reptiles, which need the warmth of the sun, can move to shade during the hottest parts of the day.

- **Hibernating** - When it's cold and snowy and there's little food available, some animals go dormant and hibernate. During the hot, dry summer months, other animals go into a similar state of dormancy, called estivation.

- **Burrowing** - Ground temperature is constant throughout the year. Animals that live in burrows get a warm place to live in the winter and a cool place in the summer. Small animals can burrow easily.

- **Cold-bloodedness** – Some animals cannot generate body heat; their bodies remain the same temperature as the environment. These animals only need one-third to one-tenth of the food that warm-blooded animals require because they don't need to generate body heat. In an arid environment, food may not be plentiful, so cold blooded animals, such as reptiles, thrive.

- **Waterproofing** - Reptiles have scaly skin and arthropods (bugs) have a hard exoskeleton to help reduce water loss.

- **Poop paste** - Water can be lost through urine, so many animals absorb that water and urinate a paste. This is common with birds and reptiles. Another strategy, used by rabbits, mice, and deer, is to poop dry pellets.

- **Migration** - Animals can migrate to a different climate, then return when weather and food availability is more favorable.

Migrating birds are a classic example.

- **Body coverings** – Feathers and hair insulate against hot temperatures and light colors reflect sunlight. The antelope ground squirrel has a large tail with a white underside. It holds its tail like a parasol over its body to protect it from the harsh sun.

What is an Animal?

Most people identify animals as creatures such as birds, frogs, and squirrels. Just don't forget worms, corals, and insects. Animals are multi-cellular, with cells organized into organs and tissues. They all must eat (plants or other animals) so have digestive systems. Animals have muscles for movement so they can search for and catch food. Any creature that moves also needs sensors such as eyes, noses, and ears to navigate, and a nervous system to control everything.

Animals in Central Oregon

Central Oregon has a wealth of wildlife and is home to many of the creatures found in arid environments throughout the American West. While we don't have unusual animals such as armadillos or manatees, the ones we have are beautiful and interesting. Let's take a look at some.

Arthropods

Arthropods are a group consisting of insects, spiders, millipedes, centipedes, and crustaceans (crabs, shrimp, and lobsters). With the exception of crustaceans, people generally consider this group to be "bugs" so, for convenience, that's what I'll call them.

Bugs have a body divided into segments with multiple legs. Their eyes are compound with many lenses, so they see the world as a mosaic. Instead of a skeleton, their body is covered with an armor-like exoskeleton. Their blood is blue because it uses copper to carry oxygen and many use their blood as a hydraulic fluid to move appendages. Most hatch from eggs, some have venom, and many can fly (not lobsters of course).

Although they are small animals, the number of bug species is greater than all other animal species combined. If you could put them all on a scale, bugs would outweigh all other animals on the planet, even when you include whales and elephants!

Many people consider bugs to be small, annoying, pests. It is true that some are harmful, but most bugs are beneficial. Insects are the primary pollinators on the planet. They produce products such as honey, wax, lacquer, and silk. Many bugs are scavengers, feeding on dead animals and plants and recycling nutrients back into the ecosystem. Bugs are also a food source for many animals. As contradictory as it sounds, bugs control pest populations (think of gardeners using ladybugs to control aphids.) Overall, bugs' benefits far outweigh any problems they cause.

Here are a few bugs you may encounter in Central Oregon:

Wasps — During the summer, you'll see wasps and yellow jackets (a type of wasp). These black and yellow insects are often found scavenging for food at picnics and in garbage cans. They collect protein, such as meat, to feed their larvae while the adults feed on nectar. They are infamous for their aggression and venomous stingers. Even worse, they can sting repeatedly (unlike bees). Despite their reputation as nasty insects, wasps are a major predator of insects, and help keep populations under control. Our wasp population fluctuates from year to year. If a warm spell in the spring is followed by a cold snap, the larvae die off, resulting in fewer wasps that year.

Juha Blomberg

Mosquitoes — Mosquitoes are the deadliest animal on the planet, killing thousands of people annually. That's because they spread diseases such as malaria, yellow fever, and West Nile virus. We're relatively safe from these dis-

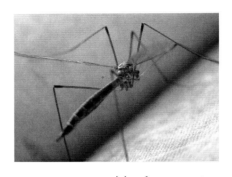

eases in the United States because most communities have vector control departments which monitor and manage mosquito populations. Twenty-five species of mosquitoes exist in Deschutes County and they can be found wherever there's a source of water for the larvae to live. Surprisingly, all adult mosquitoes eat nectar. Only the females supplement their diets with blood; they need protein to produce eggs. Using its needle-shaped mouthpart, the female mosquito injects an anti-coagulant saliva, and then sucks out blood. Our bodies have an immune system response to the saliva, which causes itching. Mosquitoes are actually good for the environment because they are a major food source for many animals, such as fish, amphibians, and bats.

Dr. David Bragg
WSU Extension

Scorpions — There are scorpions in Central Oregon, but don't worry; their sting is not very dangerous. It's about as toxic and painful as a bee sting. That's because their venom is optimized to work on insects, not humans. Scorpions use their stingers for hunting food and for defense. They are active at night and hunt other insects. During the day, they hide under rocks or in crevices. Scorpions are unique among bugs in that they give birth to live young, which hop on mom's back. Mom carries the young and cares for them until they are ready to live on their own.

Spiders — Spiders are wonderful animals that do a fantastic job of controlling bug populations. They are famous for the beautiful webs they weave to catch prey, but note that not all spiders weave webs. Some hunt using different methods. Spiders (and scorpions) are arachnids. They differ from insects in that they have four pairs of legs, no wings, or antennae. There are two species of venomous spiders in the region, the hobo and the black widow; but these spiders only bite when accidentally squeezed.

Paul Sapiano

Black widow spider.

Bark beetles — The mountain pine bark beetle bores tunnels under the bark of pine trees, feeding on the plant as well as laying eggs. The damage weakens and kills the trees, making the forest susceptible to wildfires. A healthy tree can defend itself by flooding the beetle tunnels with sap. However, beetles usually attack a tree in great numbers. In an attack, a beetle finds a mature or weak tree (both have weak defenses) and releases a pheromone to attract more beetles. This massive attack overwhelms a tree's defenses and eventually kills the tree.

Major beetle attacks happen in 70 year cycles. An infestation is currently occurring in the forests around Mt. Bachelor and Sparks

USDA Forest Service

Lake. The dying forest is filled with thousands of acres of reddish-brown tree skeletons. Fortunately, the infestation is in its final stage and will end soon. Foresters can do little to stop an infestation, but thinning Ponderosa stands helps somewhat. A major beetle attack may sound like a tragedy, but this is a natural, essential process in the forest. The beetles attack mature or weak trees, killing off an old forest to make way for a new, healthier forest.

Dead forest around Sparks Lake.

Fish

Fish are more advanced than insects, with backbones, skeletons, and advanced nervous systems. But they are more primitive than animals such as reptiles, birds, and mammals. Fish are one of the primary meat sources in the world. Here in Central Oregon fishing is an important recreational activity that also helps drive our economy.

The body temperature of most fish is the same as the surrounding environment (cold blooded). They are adapted to water, and have streamlined bodies, fins, and gills for breathing. Their bodies are covered with scales, which form an armored plating. They lay eggs, which are fertilized outside the body.

Along with the normal five senses (sight, hearing, touch, smell, taste) fish have an unusual sixth sense. An organ called the lateral line runs the length of their bodies (visible as a stripe on each side of a fish). The lateral line senses vibrations in the water, giving the fish a 3D "view" of the environment. For example, if you blindfold a goldfish (yes, scientists have done this) the fish can still navigate its tank and not bump into anything.

Central Oregon is famous worldwide for its recreational fishing for two reasons. First, many of our rivers and streams are spring-fed which offers several advantages:

- Water level remains constant year-round since the streams are not reliant on snowmelt.

- Since the water comes from underground, its temperature remains constant year-round.

- Water from springs is especially clean and clear.

Not only do these factors make ideal habitat for fish, but this consistency allows for great fishing any day of the year.

Secondly, this area is popular for the sheer variety of places to fish. Not only do we have dozens of streams and rivers, but the mountains are peppered with small lakes. Recreational fishing contributes a surprising amount of revenue to the economy of Oregon. The money fishermen spend on food, lodging, supplies, and gas contributes $500 million dollars annually to the state's economy.

The main fish found in the region are varieties of trout. The bull trout is a threatened species but the population found in Lake Billy Chinook is strong enough to allow for fishing. Redband trout are only found in the Columbia Basin and are a subspecies of rainbow trout. Eastern brook trout and brown trout are introduced species, imported in the early 1900's.

We also have a landlocked sockeye salmon called Kokanee. They can be found in lakes such as Odell Lake, Lake Billy Chinook, and the lakes in Newberry Caldera.

Bull Trout.

Instead of migrating to the ocean, these fish migrate to lakes, and then return to their home streams to spawn. In the near future, steelhead and Chinook salmon will return to Lake Billy Chinook using a new fish passage system at Round Butte Dam. This new system will allow fingerlings to travel downstream past the dam. Returning adults will be trapped below the dam and hauled up into the lake.

Amphibians

Amphibians are believed to be the first group of animals to have colonized land. They include frogs, toads, salamanders, and newts. Amphibians' lives consist of two phases; juveniles grow in water, then move to dry land as adults (Think of tadpoles turning into frogs.) Amphibians are cold-blooded, so they are sluggish and slow moving. Their jelly-like eggs are laid in water to keep them moist and are fertilized outside the body. Since they can live on land, amphibians have lungs to breathe air and legs to move around. The skin of an amphibian is thin and porous, so it must be kept moist at all times. Frogs use their skin to absorb oxygen from the air, making it their primary respiratory organ. Many amphibians have poison glands in their skin, which is why you should wash your hands after handling certain frogs and salamanders.

Because amphibians depend on water for survival, they are sensitive to chemicals in the water. Scientists use amphibian populations as an "indicator" for water quality; as water becomes polluted, amphibians are the first to die off.

Pacific tree frog — You may not see this frog, but in April, you will definitely hear it. Pacific tree frogs are famous for being noisy. In springtime dozens of frogs around ponds emit loud "ribbit, ribbit" calls to attract mates, a sound that can be heard up to a half mile away. What makes this sound so unusual is that most frogs chirp or peep. But because the "ribbit" sound is used so often in movies, most people think it represents a typical frog call.

Chris Brown

You may see these cute frogs around bodies of water. They are two to three inches long, have a black stripe near their eyes, and large, sticky pads at the ends of their toes to help them climb. They do venture away from water in search of insects. Pacific tree frogs have the strange ability to change color from brown to green or light to dark. It's not an instant change, but happens over a period of weeks depending on air temperature and humidity.

Western toad — Toads are amphibians similar to frogs but have dry, warty skin containing large poison glands. The common Western toad lives near springs, streams, meadows, and woodlands. Toads resist drying better than frogs and salamanders, making them suited to a dry environment like Central Oregon.

As tadpoles, toads eat algae and are food for predators such as fish. They grow into adults two to five inches long, and are exclusively insect-eaters. Their primary defense is the white, sticky poison produced by glands behind their eyes. It creates a nauseating, burning sensation. These toads are

Bill Battaglin

mainly active at night, but can be active during the day if nights are cold. They live in burrows, which helps them survive extreme conditions. During mating, they emit a peeping sound (like a chick) to attract mates.

Reptiles

Reptiles are more advanced than amphibians since they can live away from water. They include turtles and tortoises, alligators and crocodiles, lizards, and snakes.

Reptiles are similar to amphibians, but have more advanced adaptations for land. They lay eggs covered with a leathery, waterproof shell. This creates an interesting problem because the shell prevents fertilization. A female must be directly inseminated by the male before producing eggs. Reptiles also have lungs and a waterproof skin. Despite the perception that snakes are slimy, they actually have smooth, dry, scaly skin. Not only does this prevent water loss, but it keeps the animal very clean, since dirt can't stick. The skin doesn't grow with the animal so snakes shed their skin, peeling it off like a sock, and lizard's skin flakes off, bits at a time. Turtles and tortoises have leathery skin but also have armored shells made out of the same substance as your fingernails (their shell is modified skin).

Reptiles are cold-blooded, like most primitive animals – but with a twist. Cold-blooded animals require less food, but low body temperatures make an animal sluggish. Reptiles get around this problem by basking in the sun. As a reptile's body warms, its cells perform chemical reactions faster, allowing it to be quick and quite active (try catching a lizard on a warm day!) Of course, too much sun can cook, so reptiles move in and out of warm areas to regulate their body heat.

Importance of Reptiles

Everyone loves turtles and tortoises, but many people don't like snakes. However, reptiles perform important roles in the ecosystem:

- Rodents and insects reproduce exponentially, destroy crops, and spread disease. Without predators such as reptiles, these populations would explode, devastating ecosystems.

- Even though most reptiles are predators, they are also prey for other species such as coyotes and birds.

- Snake venom is used in medical research on blood clotting, to make anesthetics, and to produce medicines.

Lizards

Lizards are quick-moving reptiles seen scampering around rocks in Central Oregon. Most are carnivorous and eat bugs, so they are valuable in controlling pest populations. Some also eat fruits and plants, dispersing undigested seeds in their feces.

Lizards seem common and ordinary, but the next time you see one, consider these amazing facts:

- They can change color - Most lizards can subtly change their body color in response to environments or moods.

- They have three eyes - In addition to the two normal eyes, a lizard may have an opalescent gray spot on the top of its head called the parietal eye. It's a photo-sensory organ sensitive to light and dark. Even though it contains a primitive retina and lens, it can't discern images. Scientists think this organ helps lizards determine the time of day.

- Their tails can detach and re-grow – When chased, a lizard will run away, presenting its tail to the attacker. The tail has a fracture plane that allows it to snap off if grabbed by a predator. Sometimes the tail will wriggle around after breaking off, keeping the predator's attention while the lizard scampers away. Amazingly, the tail grows back.

Alligator lizard — Alligator lizards are common in Central Oregon. They look like...well...little alligators, with horny, scaly, spotted skin. These cute little guys scamper around rocks looking for spiders, snails, and bugs. Female alligator lizards are unusual in that

Marius Milner

they retain eggs in their bodies and give birth to live young when the eggs hatch.

Western fence lizard — This lizard can be identified by its bright blue belly and blue throat patches (mainly the males). They also have long toes on their back feet. They love high perches, such as fence posts, so they can sun themselves, look for food, and keep an eye on predators. Unfortunately, this location makes them easy targets for those predators. They are great at changing color, and can gradually darken (or lighten) to match their background. Like most lizards, they primarily eat bugs; so it's nice to have them in your yard. They are very territorial and do "pushups" when they feel threatened in order to expose their blue bellies (somehow this is intimidating).

Snakes

People are fascinated by snakes, whether they react with curiosity or fear. And, what's a classic western movie without the obligatory rattlesnake? Most people associate snakes with venom and striking. Yet most snakes aren't venomous. Here in Central Oregon, our only venomous snake is the Great Basin rattlesnake. But despite this snake's fearsome reputation, it's rather shy and would rather run away than strike.

As for striking, a snake moves from a coiled to a stretched-out position, so it can only strike less than the length of its body. Snakes can't leap across a room or fly through the air as movies might suggest.

How fearsome are snakes? Well, *if* you can find one, and *if* it doesn't slither away, *and* you manage to catch it, you'll probably get pooped on! Snakes poop a foul-smelling substance when caught in order to keep from being eaten. So much for fearsome…

Snakes have no limbs so they slither along the ground. Their skin is smooth and dry to repel dirt and help them slide along without snagging anything. Their eyesight and hearing are poor, but they have a highly developed sense of smell. A snake flicks out its forked tongue to gather odor molecules, then retracts the tongue and presses it against an organ on the roof of its mouth, where the molecules are "read". Some snakes, called pit vipers, have a sixth sense: they can detect the heat emitted from prey.

Snakes are carnivores. Their jaws separate, allowing them to swallow prey whole (if you had the jaws of a snake, you could swallow an entire cantaloupe.) Their teeth are pointed backwards to keep prey from wriggling out.

Some snakes have fangs and venom, both for defense and hunting. The fangs work like hypodermic syringes, injecting venom into flesh. But before you get worried about snake bites, note that in the United States, more people are killed by mattress fires than snakes!

Great Basin rattlesnake — Rattlesnakes are a classic icon of the American West, and one of four venomous snakes found in the United States. Despite their fearsome reputation, rattlers are shy and would rather run away than strike. If they feel threatened, they'll create a buzzing noise by shaking their tails. The tip of the tail contains the infamous rattle, consisting of loose buttons made of modified scales.

Allan Hack

Rattlesnake.

Rattlers feed on small animals using a "sit and wait" strategy, waiting for prey to stumble by. They have a powerful sense of smell and can detect small vibrations in the soil through their bodies. They also can detect body heat using pits located between each nostril (think of it as a kind of night vision.) Unlike constrictors, which crush prey, rattlesnakes subdue victims by injecting venom through hollow fangs. When the venom enters the prey's body, it destroys tissue, degenerates organs, and disrupts blood clotting. They may be fearsome, but rattlesnakes are eaten by birds of prey, coyotes, and king snakes.

Rattlers are shy, so it's unlikely you'll encounter one. But if you do get bitten, try to relax in order to slow the spread of venom through your body. Then get to a doctor. The doctor will administer anti-venin, a compound that counteracts the venom's action. You may have heard about other snakebite remedies, such as sucking out the venom or using tourniquets; they don't work and are actually more harmful than the snakebite. While snakebites can be serious, note that bee stings kill more people annually than rattlesnake bites.

Gopher snake — Gopher snakes are the most common family of snakes worldwide and have adapted to many climates. They are constrictors, and kill their prey by coiling around the victim and squeezing slowly until it suffocates. Gopher snakes explore burrows, rocky crevices, and even climb trees to search for food, which

Mark Bratton

Gopher Snake.

they locate by smell. They eat rodents, rabbits, lizards, other snakes, birds, and eggs. This diet helps the ecosystem by preventing quickly-reproducing rodent populations from overpopulating the area. Despite being predators, gopher snakes themselves are a source of food for hawks, foxes, and coyotes.

Since gopher snakes share habitats with rattlesnakes, they have developed a creative defense. When threatened, they coil into "S" shapes, hiss, vibrate their tails, and flatten their heads into a triangular shape, mimicking a rattler. Because their body markings are also similar to rattlers', this is enough to fool a predator. Despite this intimidating behavior, gopher snakes are harmless (well, they will poop on you if you pick one up.)

Gopher snakes are well adapted to the climate of Central Oregon. Since ground temperature remains constant year round, they live in burrows to protect themselves from extremes in temperature. In winter they hibernate, snug in their burrows from the cold. They are active during the day but in extreme heat, they become active at night.

Rubber boa — Boa constrictors in Central Oregon? Rubber boas are native to this region and are the smallest and northernmost

Bryan Harry

Rubber Boa.

snakes in the boa constrictor family. They are docile, shy, gentle, and rarely strike when handled. They have soft, shiny, brown skin and are only one foot long (they look like a rubber toy snake.) They protect themselves by hiding under logs, forest litter, rocks, or burrows. If handled, they'll simply poop a foul smelling musk.

Rubber boas are constrictors, like gopher snakes. Their main food is young rodents. Without these snakes, rodent populations would quickly explode and upset the balance of the ecosystem.

Birds

Did you know many dinosaurs were small, feathered, quick, and warm-blooded. Sound familiar? Yes, birds are thought to be the direct descendents of dinosaurs and share quite a lot of their characteristics. Here's what defines a bird:

- **Warm blooded** – Birds are quick and alert, which requires a warm metabolism in which chemical reactions happen rapidly. Birds maintain a body temperature of over 100 degrees Fahrenheit. However, this means that birds need to eat ten times more food than reptiles to fuel the furnaces that keep them warm. (I have a small parrot and he eats constantly. I guess the expression "eats like a bird" should refer to a glutton!)

- **Flight** – Birds have modified forelimbs serving as wings. Flying also requires a lightweight body. Bird bones are hollow and the feathers are extremely lightweight. Instead of carrying heavy young, they lay eggs. Water needed to produce urine is heavy, so birds reduce weight by pooping a paste instead of a liquid (usually on your freshly-waxed car).

- **Feathers** – Feathers serve several functions. They are great for insulation (which is why we fill jackets with down) and help birds maintain their high body temperature. Feathers give the bird a sleek, aerodynamic shape. Their wings consist mostly of feathers, which are lighter than flesh or bone, providing the bird with an incredibly lightweight airfoil.

- **Brains** - Flying through a forest requires excellent vision (birds can see in color). This vision is coupled with a powerful brain so the bird can analyze what it sees and quickly make flight corrections. (If someone calls you a "bird brain," take it as a compliment!)

These characteristics allow birds to avoid predators and live in places, such as cliffs, inaccessible to other animals. Birds have so much freedom that they can afford luxuries impractical for other animals such as singing loudly, remaining active during the day, and showing off colorful plumage. Their feathers display a rainbow of color, including bright blues and greens, unusual in the animal kingdom. Other animals must be quiet, secretive, often nocturnal, and have discreet earth-tone coloration to hide from predators. It's good to be a bird!

A hassle of bird life are those amazing feathers. Although useful, they require lots of maintenance. A bird spends most of the day preening, grooming every one of its thousands of feathers. During this process, it repairs feathers that have become "unzipped", cleans the feather, then coats it with oil from a preen gland at the base of its tail. The oil waterproofs the feather, keeping the bird warm, dry, and lightweight (wet feathers are heavy).

Of all the animals in Central Oregon, you will most likely see birds. There are far too many species for me to describe in this book, so

Bald Eagle.   Mourning Dove.

I'll just highlight my favorites.

Eagle — Our national bird can be seen perched regally on tree tops looking for prey, or perhaps you'll spot one flying with a fish or mouse in its talons. Bald eagles are large brown birds with distinctive, white heads, and big yellow beaks.

Mourning dove — This elegant, pigeon-like bird has soft-looking feathers, is light gray to brown in color, and has a mournful call. In flight, the feathers make a fluttery whistling sound.

Waterfowl — Mirror Pond in downtown Bend is filled with Canada geese and mallard ducks. They tip their bodies to feed on vegetation growing at the bottom of ponds (called dabbling), so you'll often see lots of goose and duck butts sticking out of the water.

Canada goose (not "Canadian goose").

Canada geese are not "Canadian" because they live all over North America. These large, black and white birds are easy to spot. They honk loudly and are bold, mildly aggressive birds. They usually migrate, but when conditions are favorable some populations remain year-round. Canada geese are particularly drawn to well maintained

Mallard.

grass lawns such as parks and golf courses. Local populations in these areas explode and the poop becomes a major sanitation problem. The city of Bend uses a special machine to lift goose droppings off park lawns. Local wildlife officials are also experimenting with anti-fertility drugs to humanely keep goose populations from growing out of control.

Mallards are the most familiar and common ducks in North America. The male is showier, with a striking, iridescent, green head. The female is a more sedate brown. Most of our domestic duck species originated from the mallard.

Steller's jay — An easy bird to identify, the Steller's jay has a blue body with a long tail, black head, and a feathery black crest on its head. Although this bird is not a "blue jay", the two are related. The Steller's jay is common throughout the west and is often found in campgrounds, boldly stealing food off picnic tables. When it's not eating

Dave Herr

Steller's Jay

123

potato chips, its diet is mainly seeds, fruits, and nuts.

Dave Herr

Northern Flicker.

Woodpeckers — Central Oregon is host to many types of woodpeckers. They are famous for banging their beaks against trees, making a jackhammer-like, tapping sound. This serves many purposes – locating insect boreholes, communication, drilling, and carving out nest holes. To feed, a woodpecker taps a tree to locate a hollow insect channel, then drills an opening, and inserts its long, barbed tongue to probe for larvae. A woodpecker's tongue is so long, that when retracted, it wraps almost around its entire skull. To prevent headaches, the bird's entire body, and especially the braincase, is designed to cushion and distribute tapping forces. My favorite woodpecker is the Northern flicker, an incredibly beautiful bird. It's large, about eleven inches long, with a spotted belly and a black crescent on its chest. It's one of the few woodpeckers that feeds primarily on the ground. In the spring, up on Awbrey Butte in Bend, you can hear woodpeckers banging on metal chimney caps to attract mates.

Quail — My favorite local bird is the California quail. They are plump, ground birds with distinctive, forward-drooping feathers on the tops of their heads. Quail are social birds that live in small groups called coveys. The alpha male usually keeps a lookout from a

Dave Herr

high perch, while the rest of the covey forages for seed, leaves, and insects on the ground below. Quail can fly, but prefer to run across the ground. In neighborhoods with a natural setting, lines of quail can often be seen scampering across the street, trailing a row of chicks that look like ping-pong balls. They nest in shrubs such as bitterbrush. If you walk by a shrub and hear a rustling noise, you probably startled a family of quail living underneath.

Hummingbirds — The rufous hummingbird is the most common hummingbird species seen in Central Oregon. These little guys have bright, iridescent plumage in shades of red, orange, and green. Hummingbirds have wings that beat fast and they can fly like a helicopter. They are the only birds that can hover, fly backwards and sideways, or travel straight up and down. They need a fast heartbeat (over one thousand beats per minute) and high metabolism to support their beating wings. Hummingbirds must eat more than their body weight of sugary nectar every day to support this metabolism and supplement their diet with insects. Although they have high-energy lives, they rest often; hummingbirds spend about eighty percent of the day perched, and at night they go into a state of partial hibernation called torpor. Because they visit flowers so often, they are important pollinators.

American robin — A common bird found throughout North

Rufous Hummingbird.   American Robin.

America, American robins can be easily identified by their orange-brown breast. They have a cheerful song and are usually the first birds to start singing in the morning. Robins are social birds, foraging for food in small groups during the day, but spending nights in large flocks. They lay bright blue eggs. Robins can be very territorial and are annoying when they decide to fight their own reflection in one of your windows. They bang against the glass for hours, making a tapping noise, leaving the window a smudgy mess.

Mammals

Mammals are pretty insignificant in terms of numbers, dominance of habitats, or variety of species. They comprise an extremely small, unremarkable side branch of the animal kingdom, lost among larger groupings such as bugs or mollusks (clams, snails, squid, etc.) Only their complex brains, the most advanced in the animal kingdom, make the members of this group stand out.

To support a complex brain, mammals have four-chambered hearts which efficiently pump blood throughout the body, supplying it with lots of oxygen. They have warm-blooded metabolisms and so must eat up to ten times more food than cold-blooded animals in order to generate heat. But warm blood allows biochemical reactions to occur rapidly, and this allows mammals to be quick, alert, and active at all times. To help retain body heat, their bodies are insulated with fur or hair which are specialized skin tissues. Mammals give birth to live young and nourish them with milk from mammary glands. The young have a long developmental period and need more nurturing because their advanced brains need time to develop.

Most mammals are small and tend to be elusive and nocturnal. Their fur is shades of brown or gray to help with camouflage (in my case, there's more gray than brown…sigh!) There are no mammals with blue or green fur. Mammals are versatile creatures and live in almost every environment. Most are land-based, but dolphins and whales live entirely in the ocean and bats fly through the air.

Below I describe a few of the mammals living in Central Oregon. Mammals are reclusive, so other than squirrels, chipmunks, and deer, you may not see very many of them. The best times to spot them are at dusk and dawn.

Humans — The most common mammals in Central Oregon are humans. We thrive in this harsh environment by using our advanced brains to manipulate tools. We build nests with central heating, wear clothing to keep warm, and import food from more temperate regions. These survival strategies enable humans to occupy almost every ecosystem on the planet.

Squirrels — Squirrels are one mammal you are most likely to see because they are active during the day. That's because they are quick and can scamper up trees to avoid predators. Squirrels are rodents (like mice and hamsters), animals with four continually growing front teeth used for gnawing. Squirrels are known for collecting seeds and caching them away, providing a steady supply of food throughout the winter. As a result, they don't need to hibernate. Forgotten seed caches sprout, helping plants spread throughout the forest. In fact, many plants rely on the industriousness of squirrels to help their reproduction. Our main types are the gray and Douglas squirrels.

Chipmunks — Chipmunks are not squirrels, though they are similar in many ways. Like squirrels, they are rodents, scamper up trees,

Squirrel.   Chipmunk.

are active during the day, and gather nuts. However, chipmunks have stripes on their faces whereas squirrels do not. Their seed caches, like those of squirrels, help the forest ecosystem by spreading seeds, helping plants get established. Chipmunks also eat fungi and spread their spores to plants. The fungi are beneficial and help plants grow. Though squirrels and chipmunks are cute, please don't feed these animals. The food you give them is not nutritious, they can bite, and some can carry diseases, such as the plague or rabies.

Marmots — Marmots are related to squirrels, but they are huge, about the size of a large cat. They can be seen near rock piles, where they build their underground dens. You may see a marmot stand up on its hind legs to survey the landscape or give out a shrieking whistle to warn others of danger (This behavior is similar to that of the unrelated  prairie dog.) Marmots eat grasses and green plants, so they must hibernate during the winter when forage is unavailable. They live in groups consisting of an alpha male, females, juveniles, and subordinate males. Marmots are my favorite mammal in the region because they are so cute. There's a colony of them along the rocky hillside near the south entrance to the Old Mill District in Bend. You'll see several of them foraging on the green lawns at the base of the hill.

Ruminants — Ruminants are animals with several stomachs, one of which is filled with bacteria that can break down hard to digest grasses. Our ruminants are mule deer, elk, and pronghorn.

Mule deer can be found everywhere in Central Oregon. Because hunting has eliminated many of their natural predators, such as wolves and cougars, deer populations are now growing beyond the food availability in the environment. A benefit of hunting is that it

Miller, NPS

JR Douglass, NPS

Pronghorn.   Mule Deer.

helps to keep deer populations under control. The rest die from starvation, are hit by cars, or attacked by domestic dogs. Deer are known for their bounding gait called "stotting". It's not as fast as running, but allows the animal to change directions quickly when being chased and helps it to see the rough landscape better.

Elk (along with moose) are the largest members of the deer family and are the largest mammals in North America. The males are famous for their large antlers which are used to ward off predators as well as for fighting during mating season. The bulls are also known for a vocalization called "bugling" used to attract mates, which can be heard for miles.

Philip Shoffner

Elk

Pronghorn antelope are the fastest animal in North America and can reach speeds of up to sixty miles per hour. Both sexes have distinctive horns (the males' can grow up to eighteen inches long.) Pronghorns are unique animals, unrelated to other antelope species, and are only found in North America. Their closest relative is the giraffe.

Bats — About twenty percent of mammals are bats and they are the only mammal exhibiting true flight (flying squirrels glide). Their wings are modified hands with leathery skin between the fingers.

Diane Probasco

Bats are famous for their echolocation ability, which they use to hunt insects in flight at night. Echolocation works like sonar; bats emit a high-pitched sound, then listen for the echo as it bounces off a target.

For some reason bats have developed a bad reputation, but they are harmless creatures. Up close, they look like a hamster with wings. American bats only eat insects or fruit. What's creepy about that? Bats are very beneficial; thousands of them eat tons of insects every night. Dusk is the best time to see bats. If you see a "bird" flying jerkily through the air at dusk, it's a bat.

Mice — In sheer numbers, the deer mouse is the most populous mammal in the world. They can be nasty pests, harboring disease and contaminating food supplies. Deer mice breed prolifically, and

John Good, NPS

produce huge numbers of offspring. Surprisingly, this is a benefit, providing a plentiful food source for predators such as birds, mammals, and reptiles. Like squirrels, mice stockpile their food, which ultimately helps plants by dispersing seeds and fungi spores.

Rabbits — In Central Oregon, you may see a cottontail rabbit or jackrabbit (actually a hare). Unlike most rabbits, which live in burrows, these guys nest above ground. Like ruminants, they eat grasses. Unfortunately, their bodies are too small to contain four stomachs, so they use a different strategy. Rabbits poop soft and hard pellets. The hard pellets are waste, while the soft pellets are eaten and digested a second time. (Yuk!) Rabbits use their long ears to listen for predators and as radiators to regulate body heat.

Dave Herr

Coyote — Nothing makes a desert night seem lonelier than the yip and howl of a coyote. Far from being lonely, the coyote is simply communicating with others of its kind. These animals are closely related to dogs and wolves, and can even interbreed with these species. Coyotes mainly eat rodents, but are versatile enough to prey on any animal, including livestock. As a result, farmers and ranchers have long tried to eliminate coyote populations. Ever versatile, the more coyotes were hunted, the faster they reproduced. As a result, coyote populations have actually increased their range throughout the United States.

Simeon Eichmann

Cats — There are two main wildcats in our region:

The cougar is the fourth-largest cat in the world (after the tiger, lion, and jaguar), and grows to eight feet in length. Cougars prey mainly on large animals such as deer and elk, but are also known to eat rodents and even insects. Attacks on humans are extremely rare because cougars generally avoid people.

Bobcats are mid-sized predators, growing up to four feet in length. They have tails with a "bobbed" appearance, the source of their name. They usually prey on rabbits and hares, but are also known to eat insects and even deer.

Cougar.   Bobcat.

Beyond Sagebrush

Other Organisms

Central Oregon is full of life forms that are neither plants nor animals. While not as obvious or showy, these organisms can still be spectacular. For example, the largest living organism on the planet was discovered in the Malheur National Forest, just east of Central Oregon. It's called a Honey Mushroom, a fungus that attacks the roots of weakened trees. Researchers determined that the fibers of this mushroom covered 3.4 square miles and figured it to be over 2,400 years old. Its weight is estimated at 605 tons, more than three times that of a blue whale. Central Oregon is definitely home to more than trees and rabbits!

In one type of classification system, organisms are divided into five different kingdoms: plants, animals, fungi, protozoa (microscopic critters that swim in pond water), and bacteria. Plants and animals have been discussed in previous chapters; now let's look at some of the other kingdoms. What are these organisms and what role do

Opposite page: Fungus growing on a dead log.

they play in our region?

Fungi

If I say "fungus" what thought first comes to mind? Perhaps athlete's foot or a moldy bathroom? Personally, I think of food because fungi are used to make wine, beer, cheese, and bread. Yum! Mushrooms and truffles are also fungi. Not bad when you think about it.

What is a fungus? At first glance, you might mistake one for a plant. But when you consider their chemistry and genetics, fungi are more closely related to animals. Since fungi don't have chlorophyll and can't perform photosynthesis, they must "eat" to survive. They do this by absorbing nutrients from plants and animals that are dead or alive. That's why mushrooms and mold thrive in the dark. So, here's an organism that's not a plant but not quite an animal.

Fungus foods. Yum!

Scientists classify fungi as a kingdom in their own right, just as important as the plant and animal kingdoms.

Four organisms make up the fungi kingdom:

- **Molds** – It's the fuzzy stuff that grows on fruit left out too long.

- **Yeasts** – These are microscopic, single-celled organisms that thrive on sugar, burping out carbon dioxide and releasing alcohol. Yeast is used to make wine and beer because it turns sugars in fruit juice or barley mash into alcohol. The carbon dioxide gives champagne and beer their bubbles. Mixing yeast with flour results in bread; the carbon dioxide makes the dough rise.

(While not yeasts, morels and truffles are included in this group.)

- **Gill fungus (mushrooms), shelf fungus, and puffballs** – These are common fungi familiar to most people.

- **Fungi imperfecti** – This miscellaneous group includes the fungi that cause disease (such as athlete's foot and ringworm), fungi used to make cheeses (such as brie), and fungi used to make drugs, like penicillin.

What's a Fungus Like?

Let's take a closer look at a typical fungus, the mushroom. Those things in supermarkets we call mushrooms are simply the "fruits" produced by a larger fungus that grows underground. The fungus itself is a mass of microscopic fibers that grow through the soil, decomposing organic matter, and then absorbing the nutrients released. This fungus can be a few miles in size and weigh several tons. Yes, you read that correctly; mushrooms are *huge*!

Just as plants produce fruit to disperse their seeds, the fungus grows thousands of mushrooms for the same purpose. Inside the cap are gills that release powdery spores. A spore is like a seed but is more durable and doesn't contain stored food, so it can be very small.

National Park Service

Typical mushroom "fruit". Notice the thousands of gills in the cap which release spores into the wind.

The mushroom cap is held up by a stem so that as the spores fall, they can be blown away by the wind.

Fungi Functions

Fungi play an important role in the environment. They are recyclers, working on the back end of the food chain, returning nutrients to the ecosystem. Plants collect energy from sunlight and produce food. Animals eat the plants and poop out the remains. The fungus takes over from there, decomposing the dung. In fact, most rotting processes are assisted by fungus, which cleans the environment of dead plants, animals, and dung. Without fungi, we'd be up to our armpits in… you get the idea.

The fruiting bodies of fungi are a source of food for animals. Humans are more creative; we eat mushrooms as food, use truffles for flavoring, and raise bread with yeast. And bizarrely, we harness the decomposing abilities of fungi to preserve food. Adding fungus to milk spoils it, producing cheese. Adding yeast to fruit juice decomposes it to wine. Adding yeast to barley mash creates beer. These products are nutritious, have a long shelf life, and they taste pretty good, too. I might as well mention that antibiotics, such as penicillin, come from mold. These aren't food but they're nevertheless an interesting product harvested from fungi.

Fungi often form partnerships with plants, helping them survive. We now understand that most plants coexist with fungi growing among their roots. The plant provides the fungus with food while the fungus absorbs water and nutrients from the soil. While a plant can live without the fungus, such a partnership greatly increases the plant's health and survival because the fungus can more efficiently absorb nutrients and water.

There is another partnership between fungi and plants. The fungi, called endophytes, grow inside the plants' leaves and stems. Not much is known about this partnership, but it seems that the fungi protect the plants from disease and maybe even from herbivores. This partnership appears to be widespread; scientists studying this concept have found endophytes in most of the plants they studied.

Fungi in Central Oregon

Beer — A place to experience fungi are the many microbreweries in Central Oregon that are gaining national attention. Again, you can't have beer without yeast!

Lichens — Lichens are a compound organism consisting of a fungus and a photosynthetic organism (either an algae or bacteria). The fungus excels at obtaining water and minerals. The photosynthetic organism uses these materials and sunlight to produce sugars, which the fungus can eat. Both parties seem to win but scientists question whether this is a true partnership or whether the fungus is simply "farming" the other organism for food.

Lichens are extremely tough and grow in places other organisms can't survive: rock outcroppings, sand, and tree bark. They can even survive the extremes of outer space! They grow whenever moisture becomes available and can operate at freezing temperatures using snow for moisture. Lichens are slow-growing due to the harsh environments in which they live. Depending on the species, they form colorful coatings or stains on rock, can be leaf-like and flaky, or look like hair.

It's commonly believed that lichens are responsible for decomposing rock into finer grains to create soil, allowing other plants to

Colorful lichens on rocks.

grow. As it turns out, this isn't true. Lichens do break down rock, but their effects are minor compared to forces such as wind, frost, and rain.

Lichens receive a lot of nutrients from dust particles in the air. As a result, they are sensitive to pollution, making them a good air-quality indicator for ecologists.

You'll see plenty of lichen on rocks throughout Central Oregon, but we also have two that commonly grow on trees. Wolf lichen is a bright yellow-green, bushy lichen that grows on the bark of trees. Native Americans used it to make dye and extracted a poison from it which they used on arrowheads. You can find lots of wolf lichen at the Cascade Lakes Scenic Highway information center, a large turnout on the road leading to Mt. Bachelor, just a few miles past the Inn at the Seventh Mountain.

Brilliant yellow wolf lichen is hard to miss.

Bryoria hangs off tree branches as a dark hairy mass. Among its common names are "Tree Hair Lichen," "Horsehair Lichen," and "Black Tree Lichen." It's edible and used as food by wildlife and Native Americans.

Mushrooms — Mushroom collecting is an unusual industry in Central Oregon. During the spring and fall harvesting seasons, hobbyists and commercial harvesters roam the forests. The US Forest Service receives $60,000-$100,000 in fees annually by selling collecting permits for these prized, edible fungi.

The commercial harvesters are migratory, following the mushrooms as they come into season. This path takes them down the Cascades then over to the coast. Dozens of species are harvested but the three most popular commercial types are the matsutake mushroom, chantrelles, and morels.

The matsutake mushroom is the most popular and can sell for $10-$100 per pound. Japan

Bryoria lichen looks like moss draped over tree branches.

is the main market for these fungi. Fortunately, we have lots of them so there are plenty to collect during the fall harvesting season. Remember the partnerships between fungi and plants? The matsutake mushroom is a good example; it forms partnerships with both ponderosa and lodgepole pines. The fungus helps the pines absorb nutrients and water from the soil while the pines provide food to the mushroom.

Protozoa

This is sort of a "catch-all" kingdom for organisms that are not quite plants, animals, or fungi. It mostly consists of single celled organisms, but it also includes more advanced organisms, such as seaweeds. Some eat like animals, others photosynthesize like plants, and some do both. Since most of these organisms are microscopic, you probably won't notice them in Central Oregon.

One worth mentioning is giardia. It exists in the environment as a dormant cyst that floats in streams and lakes. When you drink water from a contaminated source, the parasite sets up camp in your intestine and flourishes. It attaches to your intestinal wall, grows, and

produces cysts which are released back into the environment through bowel move-
ments. It takes about seven to
ten days for the parasite to
cause symptoms such as diar-
rhea, abdominal cramps, nau-
sea, and flatulence. Fortunately, there are several pre-
scription drugs available to
treat giardia.

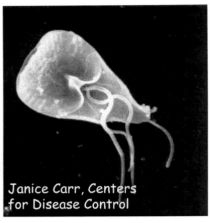

Janice Carr, Centers
for Disease Control

Giardia is one of the most
prevalent water-borne diseases
in the United States, but because of modern water treatment, you
won't get sick from tap water. A more likely cause of infection is
drinking water from lakes or streams. If you are hiking in the wilderness, bring your own water, or use a treatment system that spe-
cifically states that it can remove giardia. The most effective
method for preventing giardia is to boil your water.

Giardia parasite.

Some people believe that giardia is a modern illness. They theorize
that since more and more people are exploring the wilderness, their
activities contaminate pristine water sources. But it's more likely
that giardia has been around for some time and the water sources
were never pristine. Despite this debate, it's always best to practice
good hygiene, such as burying wastes far from streams and lakes
and washing your hands.

Bacteria

Bacteria are simple, single-celled organisms and were the first life
forms on earth. The planet is four billion years old and bacteria
have been around for the last three billion years. Despite being so
small, bacteria devastated the ecosystem by poisoning the atmosphere with a nasty, highly reactive gas called oxygen, forever
changing the environment. While deadly for primitive organisms,

oxygen was essential for the advanced biochemical processes that drive modern organisms. This resulted in an explosion of new life forms that developed over the last billion years.

Many people refer to bacteria as "germs," those nasty things in disinfectant commercials that must be eliminated from kitchens and bathrooms. But those commercials are misconceiving. First of all, doorknobs have far more bacteria than toilets. Second, most bacteria are either harmless or beneficial. For example, the bacteria on your body protect you from disease and help digest your food.

To give an idea of how important bacteria are for humans, take a look at yourself in the mirror. Of all the cells that make up your body, only ten percent are human. The rest are bacteria. The reason you see a human in the mirror is that human cells are much larger than the bacteria.

A major role of bacteria in the environment is to break down organic matter, releasing nutrients back into the ecosystem. We humans use this to our advantage in sewage treatment plants, which are essentially giant reactors filled with bacteria. Dirty water comes in one end, the bacteria eat the food scraps, soaps, and you-know-what, and surprisingly clean water comes out.

In Central Oregon our bacteria do a great job at keeping forest litter down and our sewage plants functioning. But we do have harmful

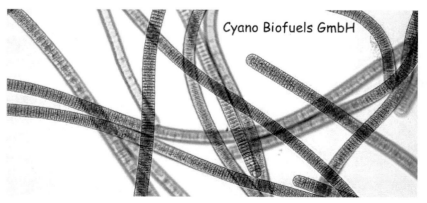

Cyano Biofuels GmbH

Cyanobacteria, also known as blue-green algae.

Algae bloom in an Oregon lake. Note the slime on the water.

ones you may encounter. Cyanobacteria (also called blue-green algae) contain chlorophyll and can perform photosynthesis. Unfortunately, when these bacteria die and decompose, their bodies release toxins into the water.

Normally, these bacteria live harmlessly in lakes throughout Oregon. But when nutrients and temperatures are just right, the populations explode, creating what's known as an algae bloom. The surface of the water turns a cloudy, blue-green color or there may be a colored slime floating on the water. The sheer numbers of organisms that are growing also mean billions are dying, their bodies decomposing, and releasing toxins into the water. Humans or pets exposed to the water may swallow or inhale contaminated droplets. The toxin damages the liver and can injure or kill.

This sounds dangerous, but it isn't something to obsess about. These are natural organisms and under normal conditions they are harmless. The state of Oregon monitors lakes and will post an advisory if a bloom is discovered. During the few days or weeks that a bloom is present, you should avoid the water – no swimming, boating, or fishing. You can still do shoreline activities such as camping and hiking. And once the bloom is over, it's safe to go back in the water. Blooms are a natural occurrence and are simply a part of the ecosystem we must learn to live with.

Biological Soil Crusts

Biological soil crusts are a good topic with which to end this chapter as they incorporate many of the organisms I've discussed. A soil crust is actually a combination of many organisms, all working together in a large colony. These organisms include cyanobacteria (photosynthetic bacteria), green and brown algae, mosses, lichens, and fungi.

Biological soil crusts are found in arid regions and grow in barren areas such as sand, gravel, or bare dirt. The organisms grow together and bind with soil particles, creating a dark lumpy mat of up to four inches thick.

These crusts have several beneficial functions. By binding with soil particles, they prevent erosion from wind and water. Their lumpy surfaces and spongy textures help catch and absorb water, helping it penetrate the soil instead of running off. The organisms within the mat convert the nitrogen in air to fertilizer and also provide minerals and nutrients for adjacent plants. Studies have confirmed that

Biological soil crust.

plants grow better with soil crusts nearby.

Because they grow on open ground, biological soil crusts are often stepped on by hikers and cattle or driven over by vehicles. The sensitive material is crushed and dies off; even one footprint is enough to kill the soil crust. These slow-growing organisms take years or even centuries to recover. Considering the benefits they provide to plants, mashing a soil crust has serious consequences.

Soil crusts can be found to the east of Bend, off of Highway 20 or in the Badlands. You may not notice them at first because they subtly blend with the surrounding soil. In undisturbed areas, look for barren patches of soil or gravel in between plants or under trees. Crusts grow in these areas and at first glance, they look like layers of decomposing leaf litter. However, the crusts are slightly darker than the soil, and upon closer inspection you'll see that they have mossy textures, lumpy surfaces, and are infused with sand. (Look in the appendix for directions to a soil crust.)

Where Do You Go From Here?

You can never get bored in Central Oregon. Thanks to our microclimates and varied geology, there's always someplace to explore and new things to learn. Hike through a ponderosa forest and imagine wildfires sweeping out the understory of bitterbrush and manzanita. The trees grow strong, thanks to helpful fungus growing among the roots. Beetles and woodpeckers feed high in the canopy while squirrels and deer forage below. Even though the Cascades block many rain clouds, summer thunderstorms water the forest. Someday, a volcano will erupt, flooding the forest with lava, perhaps making molds of the trees and leaving behind mysterious lava tubes.

I hope you've enjoyed this book, but I also hope you won't just stick it on the shelf when you finish. My intention is to excite your curiosity and inspire you to explore a favorite topic further. Are you an amateur geologist, budding birdwatcher, or do you just get turned on by plants? Whatever your interest, keep learning more about it. Here are some suggestions for getting started:

149

- Visit the places described in this book.

- Visit the High Desert Museum just south of Bend, Forest Service Visitor Centers, such as the one at Lava Butte, or your local natural history museum.

- Take a hike! It's cheap, you get lots of exercise, and you'll see stuff that piques your curiosity.

- Read books about natural history or watch documentaries on TV. Netflix has a good collection of natural history shows.

- Browse the internet – Wikipedia is a great place to start. Its information is reasonably accurate and up-to-date, especially with non-controversial topics such as natural history.

- Take a community education class through your local college or parks and recreation department.

- Finally, keep your eyes open and observe the world. If you see something interesting, learn more about it.

So, go out and explore Central Oregon!

Appendix—Driving Directions

In writing this book, my hope is that you go see this stuff for yourself. The things I discussed in the climate chapter are easy to see; just look up. For the plants and other organisms chapters, I gave general information on how to find things, which should be enough since these organisms are widespread. But I did mention a few specific locations, so I'll give directions here. Most of this section applies to formations I talked about in the geology chapter.

These directions were accurate at the time of publication. I don't expect parks and rock formations to move anytime soon, but roads, road conditions, signs, and routes can change at any time. Always double check my instructions with a current map. Note that most automotive GPS units are useless off-road; you'll see a blank map. Some locations require driving on dirt roads. These are passable for most two-wheel drive cars but still be wary. In general, be careful and note the weather; you may have to cancel plans due to ice, snow, or mud.

All of these places are wild areas even the ones that are city or state parks. Your cell phone may not have a signal. Apply the appropriate caution and common sense you'd use when away from civilization.

All directions start from the intersection of Third and NE Greenwood in Bend. Third street is the business route of Highway 97 and goes north/south. If you head east on NE Greenwood, that's Highway 20.

Plants

Awbrey Butte – Drive west on NE Greenwood for .7 miles until you reach the first traffic circle. Turn right onto NW 9th street and drive one mile to the top of the hill. This is the Awbrey Butte neighborhood and you can explore this area by turning right or left. Mistletoe is common in this area but you can also find ponderosa, juniper, bitterbrush, sagebrush, rabbitbrush, bunchgrass, mullein, dalmation toadflax, and cheatgrass. Note that the areas here are private property, so don't go farther than the sidewalk.

Century Drive/Cascade Lakes Highway – Follow the instructions for the Deschutes River trail, but don't turn at the Meadows Picnic Area. This road continues to Mt. Bachelor and beyond where you can find fir trees, wolf and hair lichen, and beetle damaged forests.

Deschutes River Trail - Drive south on NE Third Street (Business 97) for 1.5 miles and turn right onto Reed Market Road. Drive straight for 1.7 miles and turn left at the fifth traffic circle. Drive 3.3 miles along Century Drive to the sign that says "Meadows Picnic Area". Turn left onto gravel forest road 100 and follow it to the riverside parking area. There is a parking fee. The trail is on the south side of the parking lot. You will find most plants discussed in this book, with the exception of fir.

Shevlin Park - Drive west on NE Greenwood for 4.6 miles. Near the park, the road dives into a canyon. The parking area is to the left at the bottom of the canyon. You will find plants similar to what's along the Deschutes River trail.

Skyliner road - Drive west on NE Greenwood for 2.8 miles. At the fifth traffic circle turn left onto Mt. Washington Drive. Drive one mile and turn right at the second traffic circle onto Skyliner Road. If you follow the road to its end, you reach Tumalo Falls (parking fee at falls). Along this road you pass through ponderosa forest with bitterbrush, snowbrush, sagebrush, manzanita, and bunchgrass.

Soil Crusts

Drive east on NE Greenwood (Highway 20) for 13 miles. Just after milepost 13 there's a turnout on the south side of the road. If you explore on the north side of the road, you'll see soil crusts. You can also find soil crusts if you explore Dry Canyon or the Badlands.

Geology

Note: You may want to combine Hole in the Ground, Fort Rock, and Crack in the Ground into one trip. It's a long drive and the three sites are close to each other.

Crack in the Ground - Follow the instructions for Ft. Rock. When you reach the town of Ft. Rock, continue straight and stay on the main road (it will turn south). Turn left onto Christmas Valley/Wagontire Road and drive to the town of Christmas Valley. Drive through town and as you are passing the airport, look for Crack in the Ground Road on your left. Turn left onto the road and drive about 8 miles to the parking area. Note that the pavement will end, but the road continues as a dirt road, BLM road 6109 to the parking area.

Dry Canyon/Badlands - Head east on NE Greenwood (Highway 20) for 17 miles and turn left onto a small paved road. Make an immediate right onto a dirt road and drive past the gravel piles until you can go no further. From here you'll have to hike into the canyon. Contact the BLM to see when the canyon is open for hiking. An alternative - continue on Highway 20 another mile or so to a turnout with a view of the canyon. For the Badlands, after you turn off the highway, stay on the paved road and follow the signs.

Fort Rock - Drive south on NE Third (Business 97) for 3.2 miles, then turn left (south) onto Highway 97. Drive south on Highway 97 for 28.4 miles. Just after milepost 169, you'll see the signed turnoff (Silver Lake/Lakeview) onto Highway 31. Turn left and follow Highway 31 for 29 miles until you reach milepost 29. Turn left at the signed intersection (Ft. Rock/Christmas Valley) and continue to the tiny town of Ft. Rock. Just past the town, turn left onto Cabin Lake Road and follow it to the park entrance.

Hole in the Ground - Drive south on NE Third (Business 97) for 3.2 miles, then turn left (south) onto Highway 97. Drive south on Highway 97 for 28.4 miles. Just after milepost 169, you'll see the signed turnoff (Silver Lake/Lakeview) onto Highway 31. Turn left and follow Highway 31 for 22 miles until you reach milepost 22 and a sign that says "Breakup Road/Hole in the Ground". Turn left onto the dirt road and follow it for 4.4 miles. There are three forks in this road. Turn right at the first two forks and left at the third.

Lava Lands Visitor Center and Lava Butte Cinder Cone - Drive south on NE Third (Business 97) for 3.2 miles, then turn left (south) onto Highway 97. Continue south for 7.7 miles and take the visitor center exit just past milepost 149. Turn right at the end of the off-ramp. There is a fee to park.

Lava Cast Forest - Drive south on NE Third (Business 97) for 3.2 miles, then turn left (south) onto Highway 97. Drive south on Highway 97 for 11.2 miles and take exit 153 to South Century Drive. Turn left at the stop sign and drive straight ahead to Forest Service road 9720 (there will be a sign for Lava Cast Forest). Continue on this dirt road for 9 miles until you reach the parking area. There is a fee to park.

Lava River Cave - Follow the instructions for the Lava Lands Visitor Center but go straight when you get to the end of the off-ramp. Drive about 100 yards and turn left onto the road that goes under the freeway (The road is marked with a sign for Lava River Cave.) Drive one mile to the cave parking lot, on the right. There is a fee to park. The cave is free if you bring your own flashlights, but they do rent lanterns.

Newberry Crater - Drive south on NE Third (Business 97) for 3.2 miles, then turn left (south) onto Highway 97. Drive south on Highway 97 for 20.3 miles. Just after milepost 161, you'll see signs for Newberry Caldera directing you to the turnoff on your left. After turning, drive up the road about 13 miles until you reach the caldera. There is a fee to park.

Pilot Butte Cinder Cone - Drive east on NE Greenwood (Highway 20). In the summer, you can drive to the top. Just before the butte, make a left turn onto the marked access road. In the winter, this road is closed. Continue past the butte and make a left turn onto NE Azure Drive, left on NE Savannah Drive, and left on NE Linnea Drive. Continue straight until you reach the parking area for the foot trail to the top.

Smith Rock - Drive North on Highway 97 for 22 miles to Terrebonne. Turn right at the flashing light and follow the signs to Smith Rock State Park. There is a parking fee.

About the Author

Darin Furry has explored and hiked throughout Oregon, Washington, and the Southwest. He's worked as a Park Ranger in the Columbia River Gorge and has a degree in Biology from the University of California, Davis. He currently lives in Bend.